THE RESIDENTIAL PARKS of TUNBRIDGE WELLS

by
Members of the Local History Group
of the
Royal Tunbridge Wells Civic Society

Edited by
John Cunningham

Royal Tunbridge Wells Civic Society
Local History Monograph No. 4

Published by
The Royal Tunbridge Wells Civic Society
2004

**Published in Great Britain in December 2004 by
the Local History Group of
The Royal Tunbridge Wells Civic Society**

ISBN No. 0–9545343–3–6

The text is set in Bookman Old Style 10pt. and the front cover in Bookman Old Style 16pt.

Front cover: Part of Nevill Park seen from Hungershall Park
Back cover: No.1 Camden Park
Title page: Nevill Park

Printed and bound by the Ink Pot Lithographic Printers,
Southborough, Tunbridge Wells, Kent TN4 OLT

CONTENTS

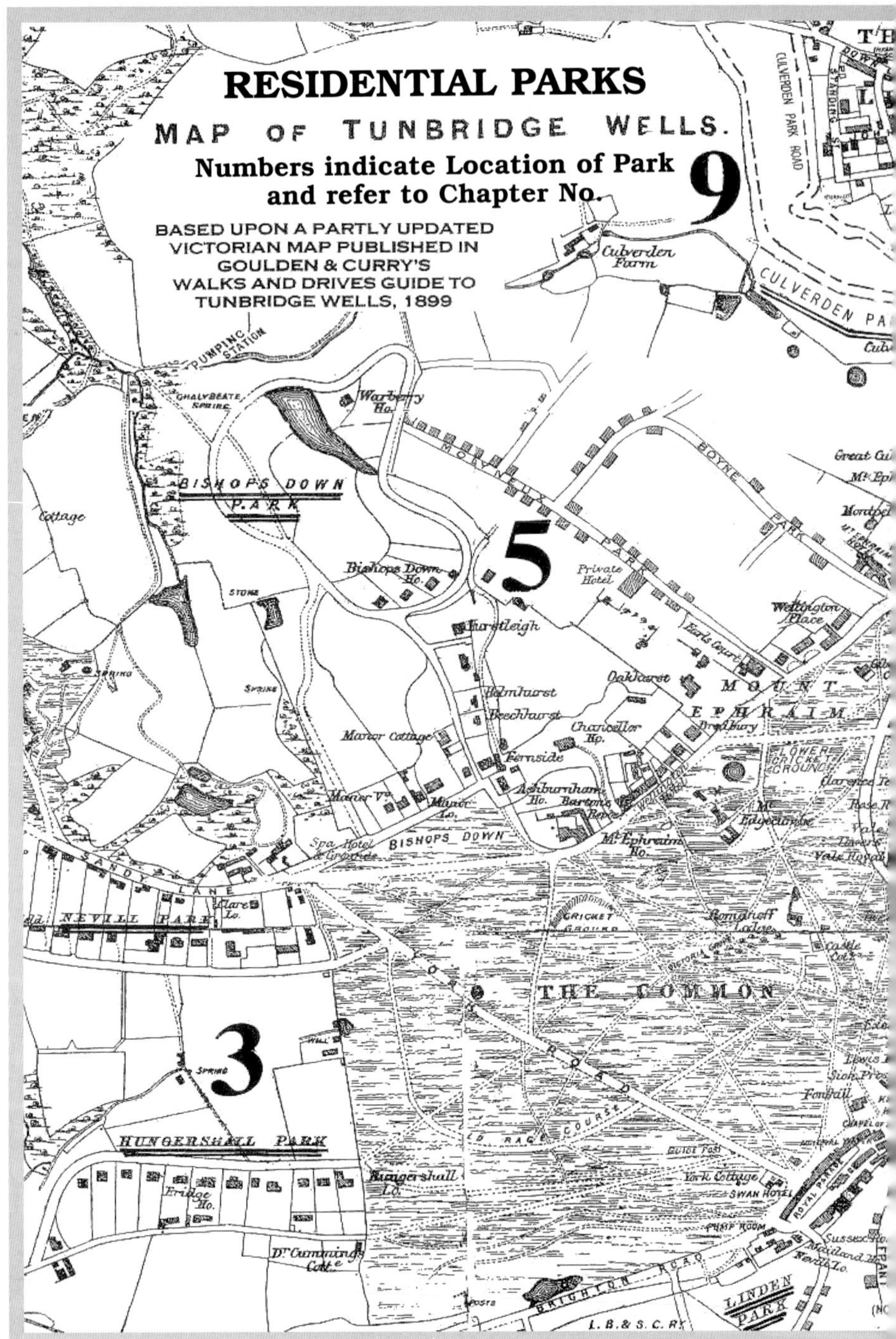
RESIDENTIAL PARKS
MAP OF TUNBRIDGE WELLS.
Numbers indicate Location of Park
and refer to Chapter No.
BASED UPON A PARTLY UPDATED
VICTORIAN MAP PUBLISHED IN
GOULDEN & CURRY'S
WALKS AND DRIVES GUIDE TO
TUNBRIDGE WELLS, 1899
9
5
3
CULVERDEN PARK ROAD
Culverden Farm
PUMPING STATION
CHALYBEATE SPRING
Warberry Ho.
BISHOPS DOWN PARK
MOLYNEUX PARK
BOYNE PARK
Cottage
Bishops Down Ho.
Private Hotel
Wellington Place
Earls Court
MOUNT EPHRAIM
Oakhurst
Holmhurst
Beechhurst
Chancellor Ho.
Manor Cottage
Fernside
Ashburnham Ho.
Manor Lo.
Spa Hotel & Grounds
BISHOPS DOWN
Mt. Ephraim Ho.
Mt. Edgecumbe
SANDY LANE
NEVILL PARK
Clare Lo.
CRICKET GROUND
Romanoff Lodge
THE COMMON
SPRING
HUNGERSHALL PARK
Eridge Ho.
Hungershall Lo.
OLD RACE COURSE
GUIDE POST
York Cottage
SWAN HOTEL
PUMP ROOM
ROYAL PARADE
Dr. Cummings Cott.e
BRIGHTON ROAD
L. B. & S. C. RY.
LINDEN PARK

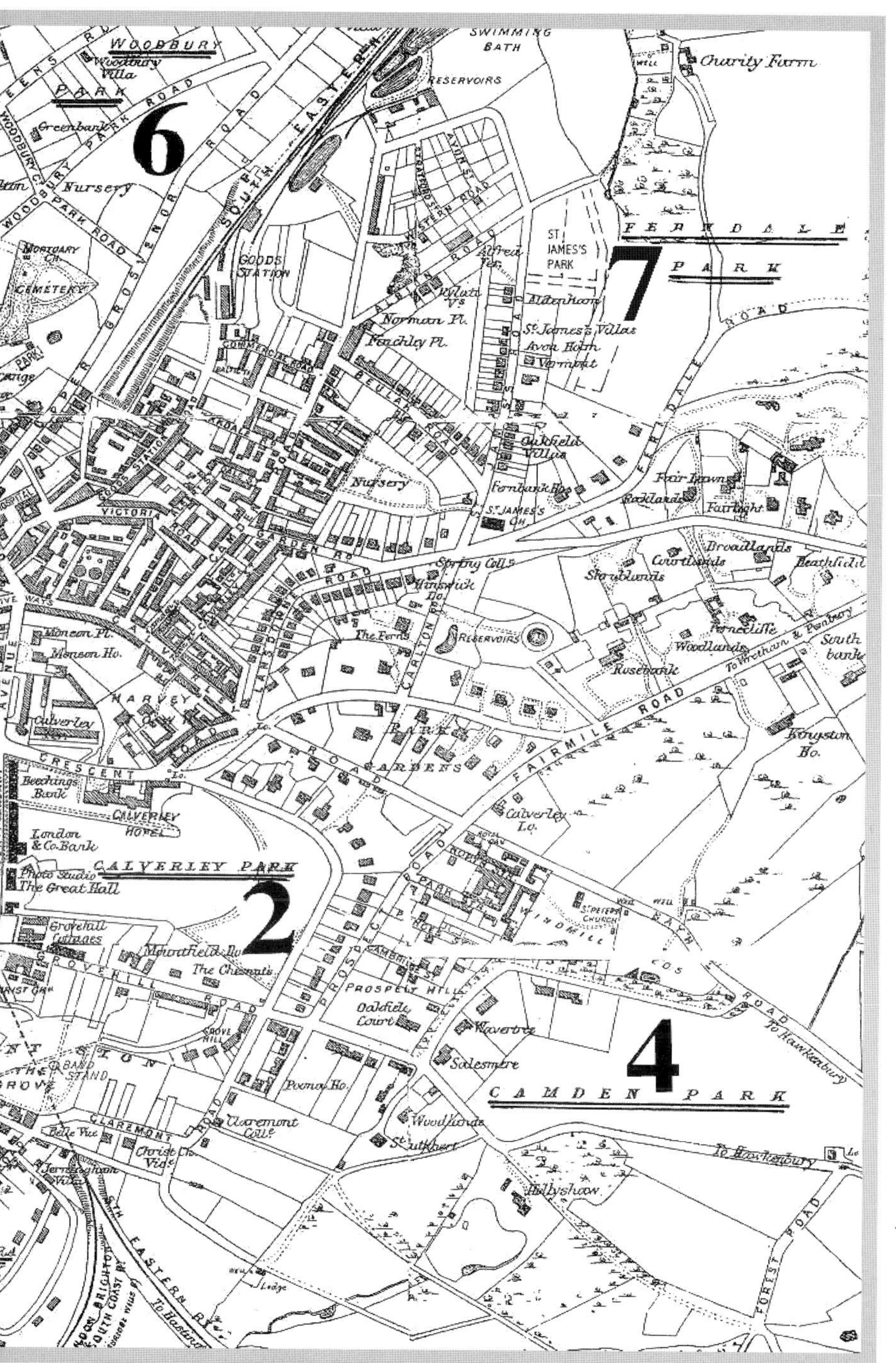
WOODBURY
PARK
6
7
FERNDALE
PARK
2
CALVERLEY PARK
4
CAMDEN PARK
Charity Farm
Swimming Bath
Reservoirs
Goods Station
Cemetery
Nursery
St. James's Park
St. James's Ch.
Victoria Road
Garden Rd
Fairmile Road
Crescent
Calverley Hotel
The Great Hall
Prospect Hill
Grove Hill Road
Band Stand
Claremont
To Hastings
To Hawkenbury
Forest Road

Pembury Grange, Sandown Park designed in 1869 by the noteworthy architect George Devey, FRIBA.

INTRODUCTION

In the year 1828, the talented architect, Decimus Burton, brought London's Regent's Park concept of villas in a landscaped setting, to John Ward's Calverley Estate in Tunbridge Wells, and Calverley Park was born.

Other landowners in Tunbridge Wells soon followed suit, and by the end of the 19th. century, the town of Tunbridge Wells was ringed by residential "parks", as the map on page iv and v shows.

The earliest of these parks were spacious villas set in parkland, while later ones had smaller open spaces and even later, they were 'only' sylvan roads. Despite pressures for change, Tunbridge Wells continues to owe much of its pleasing character to these 19th. century parks.

During the 1970s and 1980s, the Society arranged a series of 'walks' around these 'parks', led by Geoffrey Copus and myself. Notes for these walks have remained the most authoritative source of information on the areas concerned for a generation.

The subject of the ' parks' is seminal to the history of Tunbridge Wells and when this new series of monographs was devised, it was clear that this important aspect of the town's history needed to be updated. Consequently, Geoffrey and Brenda Copus have updated their previous research and other members of the RTWCS Local History Group have added their assessment of other parks.

We are, however, all aware that this monograph merely 'skates over the surface' of the subject of 'The Residential Parks of Tunbridge Wells'. Each Park deserves a separate monograph in its own right and it is to be hoped that several will have their own in due course.

I should like to acknowledge my appreciation of Mary Woodruffe who has typed impeccably my own contribution; and to John Cunningham, the Secretary of our Local History Group, who has edited this monograph and seen it through production in his usual efficient way.

Dr. Philip Whitbourn, OBE
Chairman, RTWCS Local History Group
President, Royal Tunbridge Wells Civic Society
November 2004

CHAPTER 1

THE CONCEPT OF THE RESIDENTIAL PARK

by John Cunningham

Residential parks are an urban rather than a rural concept. They did not exist before the early part of the 19th. century; and Tunbridge Wells was to play a significant part in the development of the concept.

Urban parks and gardens however owe their origins very much to the countryside and to people's desire to bring the beauty and values of the countryside into the town – to create *rus in urbe.*

Historically, the development of parks and gardens has been essentially a function of three social conditions – a stable peaceful society; the leisure to enjoy parks and gardens; and the disposable income to afford them.

In the Middle Ages, none of these conditions existed. But the seeds of the Park and the Garden were to begin to germinate then.

It is no coincidence that the words 'Park' and 'Garden' are of Norman, rather than Anglo-Saxon origin, reflecting both the dominance and the life-style of the conquerors. The very first Parks were deer parks: in effect, enclosed woods or even forest to make hunting easier and more controllable. Naturally such Parks were only for the Lords of the Manor and certainly not for ordinary folk.

As life became more peaceful and settled, and castles were replaced by fortified manor houses and then by manor houses, the idea of a garden began to develop – first as the practical 'kitchen' garden, to supply vegetables and fruit for the Lord of the Manor's table; and then as the more decorative 'flower' garden for the leisure of the Lord and his Lady and for their socialising. Both of these can be seen in paintings and in Books of Hours of the 15th and 16th. centuries. They were, however, very much an aristocratic and rural custom; and certainly not middle-class or urban.

There was obviously a strong Continental, particularly French influence in the development of the garden and this probably accounts for the precision and formality of design which was a feature of early gardens. There was, however, to be a transition from the formal gardens and clipped hedges of the 17th. and early 18th. centuries to more natural picturesque landscape gardening in the mid-18th century; what Mark Girouard calls 'the Arrival of Informality' between 1770-1830.

Axial planning – straight avenues, canals and walks – gave way to circular planning – a circuit which revealed vistas, temples, and obelisks in natural settings. This was the origin of the English Park, a largely home-grown development, which was much admired and copied in Europe. Lancelot (Capability) Brown (1716-1783), Humphrey Repton (1752-1818) and Joseph Paxton (1801-1865) were prime influences in this.

Part of this change to an English Park – a larger, landscaped park – was practical and economic. If one was going to increase the size of one's park for whatever reason – status, fashion, increased wealth – it was nonetheless very expensive to do so, if it was to remain a formal park. It was much less expensive to convert agricultural land into pastoral landscaped scenery.

But a larger part of the change was one of taste and mood. The landscape gardening movement coincided, and integrated itself, with the so-called Romantic Movement in literature (a name incidentally not coined until after the period had ended). Both movements represented a reaction against an over-formalised structure, with a desire to return to nature, to past times, to vague memories of Utopia. This desire to escape (or was it retreat?) into ideas of 'Arcadia', was possibly encouraged by the increasing uncertainties of life in the second half of the 18th. and the beginning of the 19th century.

The uncertainties created by the Seven Years' War (1756-1763), the American Revolution (War of Independence)(1776-1783), the French Revolution (1789-1795), the Napoleonic Wars (1796-1815), and the Peterloo massacre of 1819 suggested to many that life and society were increasingly volatile and were changing fast, maybe too fast for some.

The 'Industrial Revolution' was also taking place at the same time. It was actually more evolution than revolution, but it nonetheless turned society upside down. It enabled huge increases throughout Britain in productivity, as well as in physical and social mobility, the latter particularly helped by the coming of railways late in the 'Revolution'. Almost inevitably this led to a greater awareness of, and a sharpening of the divisions between, the classes.

There was also an Agricultural 'Revolution' in Britain in the 18th century as landowners were changing from being rentiers, which in effect was what the feudal system had been, to running their own estates and making 'improvements' in cultivation, crops and productivity.

At the same time, there was a considerable development of turnpike roads, with a corresponding improvement in the design and speed of stagecoaches and eventually in the early-mid 19th. century, there was the arrival of the railways.

All of which made the country and countryside less remote and the idea of Arcadia more approachable, desirable and obtainable; and the Park, the English Park, was to become its quintessential expression.

Parks had of course existed since the 16th, century in the ultimate English 'town' – London – as 'Royal' Parks , often but not always associated with Royal palaces: St. James', Green Park, Hyde Park, Kensington Gardens. In the 17th. century, London had also copied the idea of the Square first from the Italian Piazza and then from France and particularly the Place Royale [Place des Vosges] in Paris, which introduced the idea of a square having a central garden enjoyed by all.

It was not too large a jump from such a Square to a larger residential Park which brought in even more of the countryside. The first residential Park in London was Regent's Park. Its 500 acres had been a Royal hunting park since Henry VIII, and it was only in 1811 that the terraces, crescents and villas which we know today were first planned by John Nash as the culmination of his planned 'royal' route from Carlton House Terrace through Waterloo Place, Lower Regent Street, Piccadilly Circus, Regent Street, Oxford Circus and Portland Place to Regent's Park. The Park itself took from 1812 to 1828 to develop and even so only 8 of its planned 56 villas were built, but it had a profound effect on architectural thinking and public taste. Decimus Burton played an integral part in its development, as he was to do not much later from 1828 in Tunbridge Wells.

So it is not surprising that when new upper-middle class houses were planned in the 19th. century, the attraction of a residential Park, based on the 18th. century concept of an English Park, was well-accepted, and the planners should seek to create 'rus in urbe' and transfer what they saw as Arcadia, although on a more modest scale, to new developments, such as in Tunbridge Wells.

Transferring the concept of a Park from the country to a city or town, obviously meant a reduction in size. But there was a pleasing illusion that although the Park was shared with other residences, it looked from each residence as if it belonged just to you.

The nature of the Park also changed. Not only was it smaller, but its audience were urban 'sophisticates' who wanted a 'romantic' backdrop to, but not a controlling influence on, their lives. So the muck, sweat and tears of country life was eliminated.

The original concept of the residential Park was, however, to be changed and modified over time, as it filtered down the social classes.What started with the urban upper middle class as properties with a shared miniature, but real, park, turned with the middle classes into properties with wide roads and large gardens, and finally with the lower middle classes into a pleasant residential road which called itself 'Park'. The interval between the first and the last stage was only about 70-80 years. The influence of 'hype' (even in the 19th. century) and the commercial interests of the property developer in this, should not be underestimated.

This change can be clearly seen in the development of Tunbridge Wells.

There are today twenty-eight streets/areas in Tunbridge Wells with the title 'Park'. However only seven of them have a 'park' as such: Calverley, Nevill, Camden, Hungershall, Bishop's Down, Molyneux, Culverden; and a further eight are wide roads and often large gardens and a sylvan setting, namely: Boyne, Grosvenor, Linden, Madeira, Sandown, Sandhurst, Warwick and Woodbury.

These 15 are the subject of this monograph.

CHAPTER 2

CALVERLEY PARK

Including Calverley Park Gardens and Calverley Park Crescent

by Philip Whitbourn

"A landmark in English domestic architecture" is how the late Christopher Hussey once described Calverley Park, in the pages of "Country Life" magazine, "on the precedent of Nash's original layout of Regent's Park." (1)

Nash's original vision for Regent's Park was for a Reptonian landscape in which each of the fifty-six villas mentioned in Chapter 1 of this Monograph would be so sited as to be out of the sight of its neighbours, so that all would enjoy the illusion of appearing to be in sole enjoyment of the whole park.

Of the eight villas actually built in Regent's Park, the young Architect Decimus Burton (1800-1881) designed six, and had a hand in the other two. Decimus Burton was also involved in the design of Cornwall and Clarence Terraces in Regent's Park, the leases on the latter property being held by investor John Ward, for whom Burton designed a mansion called Holwood in 1823-6. This was set in a park that had been landscaped by Repton and it is situated between the villages of Keston and Farnborough, near Bromley.

By the end of the year 1826 Ward was also in possession of the 874 acre Calverley Estate of mainly farmland at Tunbridge Wells. One interpretation of the name Calverley has been as "calves lea or meadow", and the name has been around in Tunbridge Wells since Stuart times (2).

In 1828, Burton produced a layout for building development on 56 acres of the Estate, at

Calverley Park Villas, arranged in an arc along a curved carriage drive.

its eastern end. The greater part of this first phase of development was taken up with Calverley Park, where a sequence of single and paired villas were arranged in an arc, set back from a curved carriage drive. The windows of the principal rooms in each villa looked out over pleasure grounds and a "ha-ha" towards the valley below (now Calverley Grounds), again giving the illusion of sole enjoyment of ancestral acres of parkland.

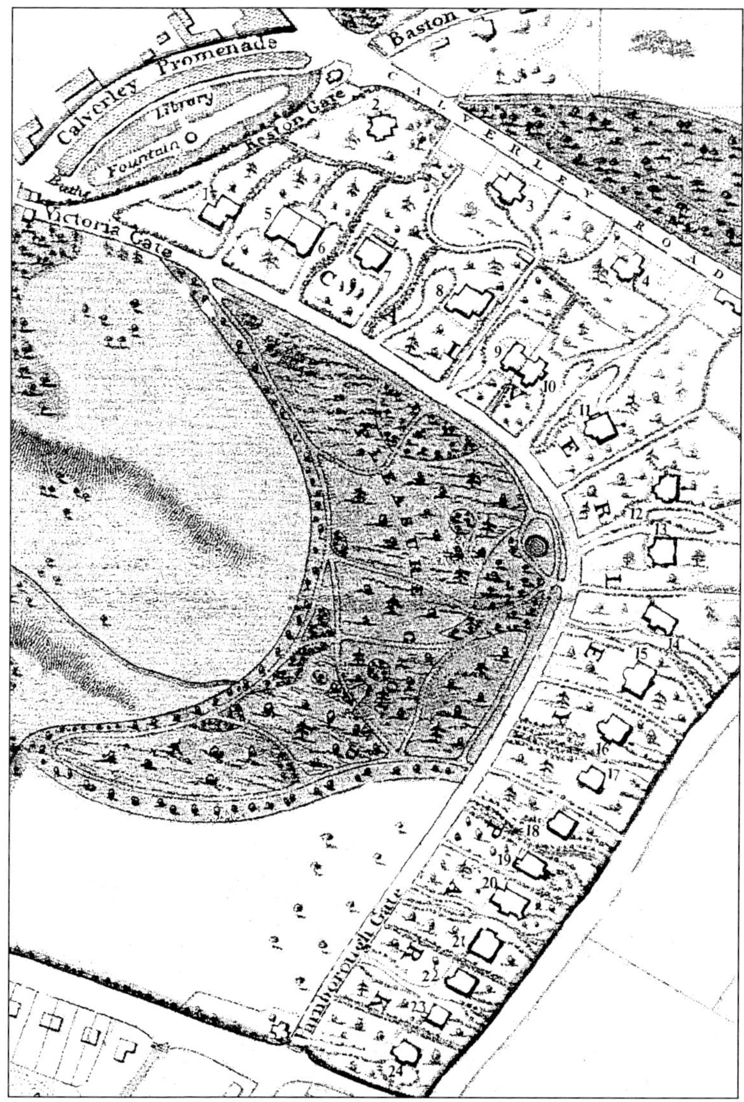

Calverley Park in the 1830's. showing the arc of villas overlooking the pleasure ground.

Moreover, the gardens of several of the villas were interesting examples of miniature picturesque landscapes in their own right. At No.7, for example, the garden elevation of the house itself is a symmetrical composition with, like Holwood, a semi-circular bow as its central feature. However, the windows of the principal rooms, the Drawing

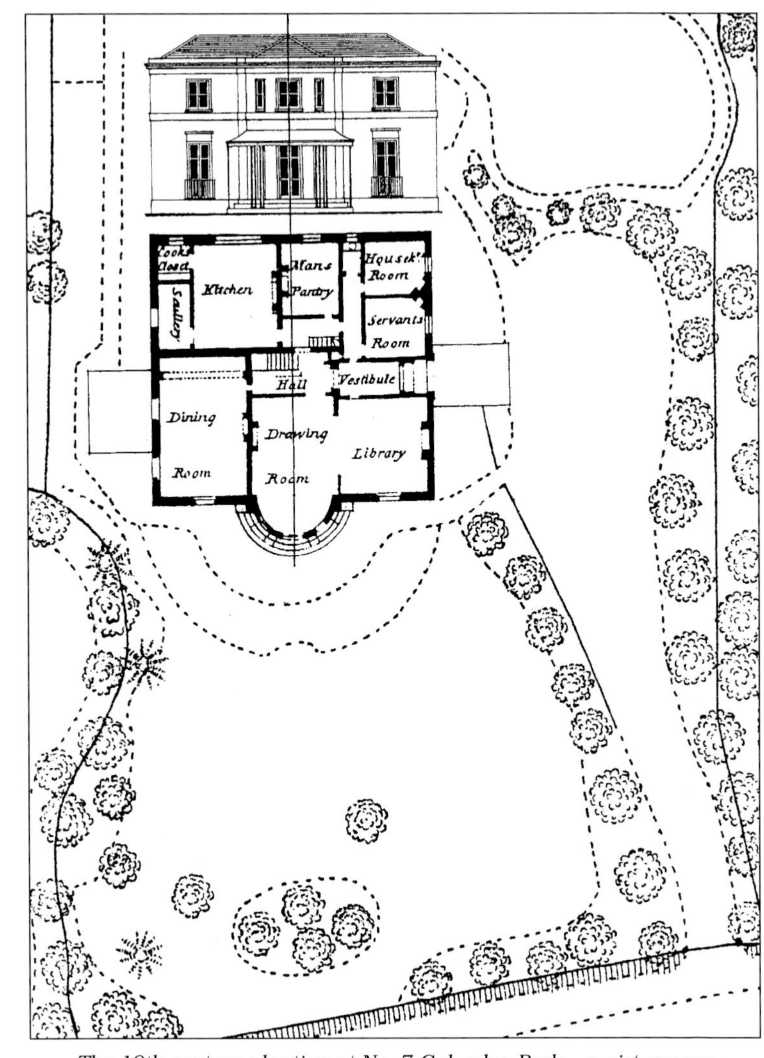

The 19th century planting at No. 7 Calverley Park – a picturesque landscape in miniature.

Room, the Library and the Dining Room do not look out on to a formal avenue framing the view beyond, but on to informal curved lines of planting and interspersing single trees or clumps.

In some instances two villas share an access way from the carriage drive, thus reducing the amount of the landscape given over to hard surfacing. The access way between Nos. 12 and 13, illustrated below is a case in point.

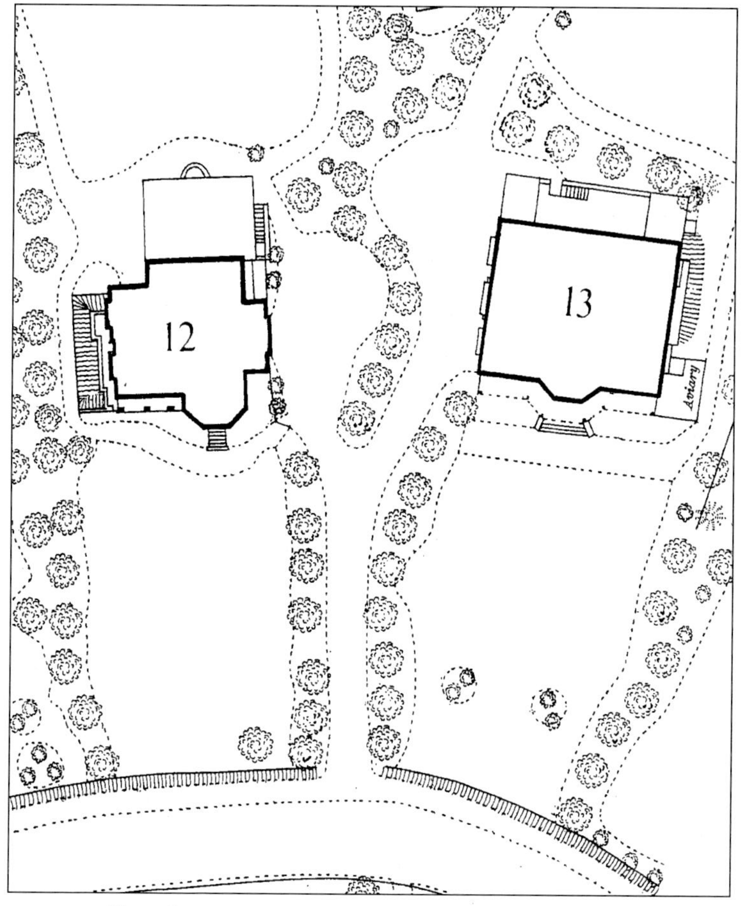

Shared access way to Nos. 12 and 13 Calverley Park.

Burton's original design for Calverley Park envisaged rather more villas, between 30 and 40 in all, including some on the land between the Pleasure Ground and Grove Hill Road, which came to be developed later.

Thanks, initially, to enlightened management by the Ward Estate and, more recently, to Listed Building and Conservation Area controls, the whole layout of twenty-four villas as built, together with the three lodges, remains substantially intact.

ARCHITECTURAL STYLES IN CALVERLEY PARK

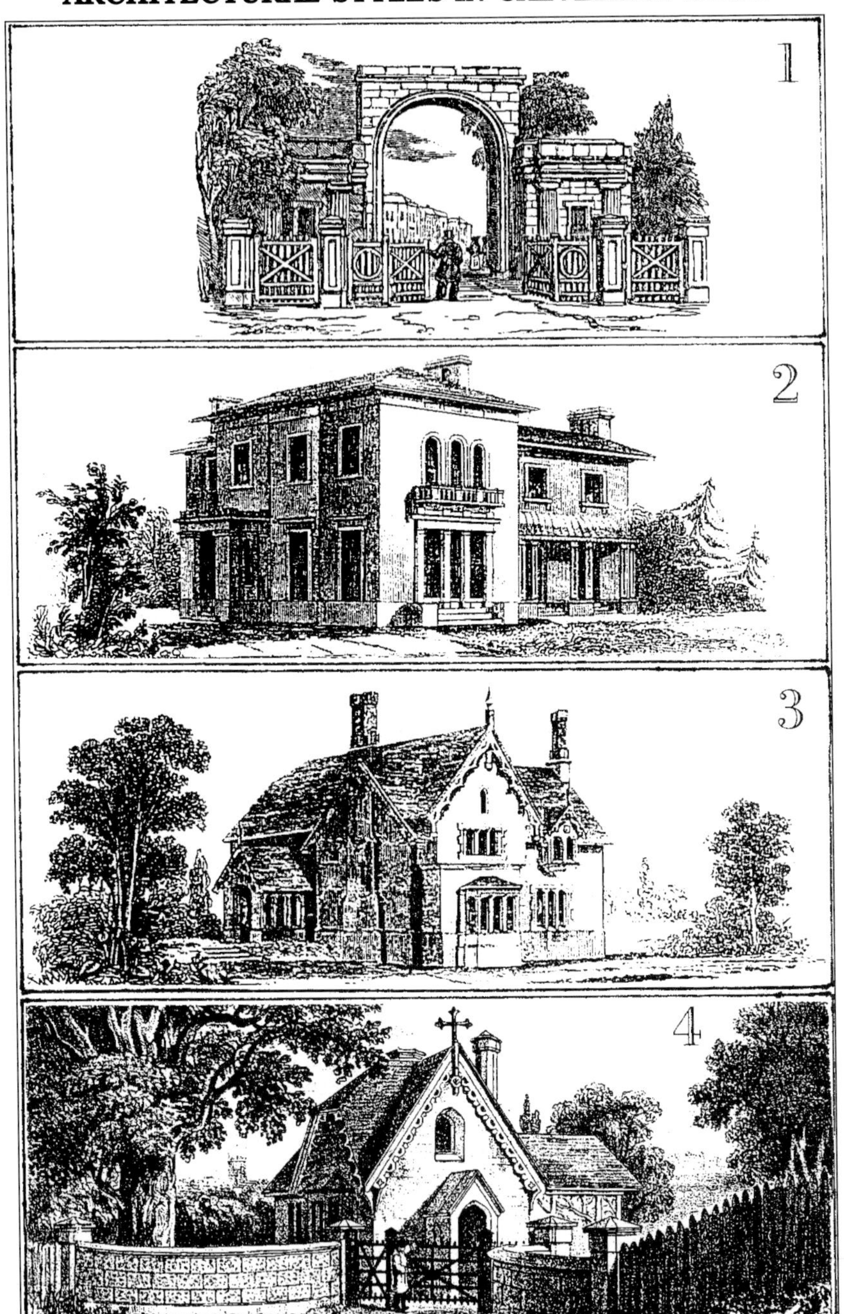

1. Grecian 2. Italianate 3. Old English 4. Gothic

The harmony of the group of buildings at Calverley Park depends partly upon the use throughout of the locally quarried sandstone, and partly upon consistency of scale, for there are considerable variations in architectural style.

A Greek Doric Order features on Victoria Lodge, and Italianate details, such as triple windows and bracketed eaves, at Nos. 1, 8, 17 and 23. Nos. 3 and 4 are "Old English" in character, with high-pitched roofs, decorative bargeboards and Tudoresque details, while Nos. 12 and 24, together with Farnborough Lodge, have "Gothick" touches, with the use of pointed arches. Keston Lodge and Nos. 2, 5, 6, 9, 10, 11, 13, 14, 15, 16, 18, 19, 20, 21, 22 and 23 are, like No.7, "Regency" style classical buildings in the late-Georgian tradition.

The builder/developer of Calverley Park was the London firm of Messrs. Bramah of Pimlico, who set up workshops in Tunbridge Wells for the purpose, and took out building leases. (2) Building started from the Victoria Lodge end towards the close of the 1820s and was complete by the end of the 1830s. The houses were not particularly large by the standards of the time, although some, such as No.12, were extended later in the 19th century. Others which had basement kitchens originally, had kitchen extensions added later.

John Ward's two sons, Arthur Wellesley Ward and Neville Ward lived, respectively, at Nos. 11 and 13, while Decimus Burton himself took possession of No.4 for a while in 1835.

The 1851 census shows No.7, illustrated on page 8, to be occupied by Miss Elizabeth Hawley, daughter of Sir Henry Hawley, together with her brother, the Revd. James Hawley and his wife Henrietta. The domestic staff numbered five: a Butler, a Housekeeper, a Ladies Maid, a Housemaid and a General Servant. At No. 20, Lady Georgina Pratt had three servants and a footman. Some other houses, however, were intended to be run by two or three servants.

Probably best known of Calverley Park's former residents was Air Chief Marshal Lord Dowding, (1882-1970) who was in charge of Fighter Command when the crucial Battle of Britain raged over Kent's skies at the start of the Second World War. An earlier resident of No.1 was Sir Ifor Evans, subsequently Baron Evans of Hungershall (1899-1982), Provost of University College, London, from 1951 to 1966. Other residents of note include Sir Willaim Wigham Richardson at No. 4; Lady Lloyd at No. 12; Sir Horace Williamson at No.14; Lady Wray at No.16; Lady Parker at No.17; and the architect Cecil Burns at No.11.

There can be no doubt that Decimus Burton's work at Calverley Park is of seminal importance in the history of Tunbridge Wells. It was not just that he created "A landmark in English Domestic architecture". Tunbridge Wells' first residential park established an architectural and landscape character that came to be emulated in various ways in the area around, and thus established an architectural and landscape character that remains a prominent feature of the town to this day.

Closely associated with Calverley Park, and forming adjacent parts of Decimus Burton's layout, are Calverley Park Crescent and Calverley Park Gardens.

Calverley Park Gardens.

Originally known as Calverley Plain, Calverley Park Gardens was laid out by Decimus Burton in 1828 at the same time as Calverley Park. The stone retaining wall facing Calverley Park across Calverley Road formed part of Burton's scheme. Behind this, James Phippen tells us in Colbran's New Guide of 1840, some extensive pleasure grounds similar to those in Calverley Park itself, were "laid out with great taste".(4)

Subsequently, these have been subsumed into the gardens of the original villas on the south side of the roadway, although the area that these pleasure grounds once occupied remains mostly sylvan and unbuilt upon.

Of the villas on the north side of the roadway, No.3, The Hollies, appears to be the earliest and has been attributed to Burton, being similar in appearance to the stone-faced Calverley Park villas. No.5, Sandhurst Lodge made its appearance in the local Rating and Finance

Decimus Burton's No.3 Calverley Park.

William Willicombe's No.7 Calverley Park Gardens.

Committee in 1855 under the name of Willicombe; No.7, Beech Holm in 1854; No.9, Galloway House in 1859. No.11, Stenton Lodge, is also are by William Willicombe, whose name features in a surviving Indenture of Release.

A Town Commissioner, William Willicombe (1800-1875) was a contemporary of Decimus Burton and worked with him on the development of Calverley Park, before undertaking developments in Tunbridge Wells on his own account. The Willicombe Villas on the north side of the roadway are of red brick with stone quoins and dressings and they have steeply pitched roofs, with some surviving decorative bargeboards.

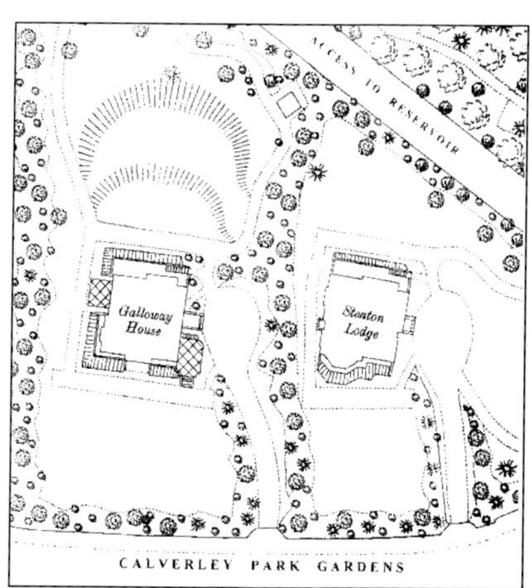

Nos. 9 (Galloway House) and 11 (Stanton Lodge), Calverley Park Gardens, showing the informal landscape settings.

As may be seen from the plan on this page, the landscape setting of the villas is, like that in Calverley Park, informal. The villas on the south side of the roadway, No.4, Lansdowne; No. 6, Braffords; Nos. 10 and 12, now Highlands House, and sometime Tunbridge Wells Maternity Home; No.14 and No. 16, Wissenden, are stucco-faced in the classical style.

An Indenture of 3rd. November 1851 stated that buildings on the north-east side of the roadway should be detached villas of no less value than one thousand pounds and set in grounds of at least three-quarters of an acre. Also, front fences were to be set back seven feet from the footpath, allowing for the planting of hollies and shrubs, a feature that still contributes to the character of the road.

Sadly, Decimus Burton's own 'cottage-orné' residence at No.2 was demolished over a century ago. It features on the left-hand side of the 1831 illustration below, with No. 2 Calverley Park, Keston Lodge, and Victoria Lodge beyond. Also shown in this view is Baston Gate, through which the roadway was approached from what is now Carr's Corner.

Calverley Park Gardens, looking towards Calverley Park, 1831.
L to R: Decimus Burton's Cottage Ornée "Baston Cottage"; Baston Lodge; No. 2 Calverley Park; Keston Lodge; Victoria Lodge.

At the time of this illustration, Calverley Park Crescent, or Calverley Promenade as it was originally called, was still at the proposal stage.

The houses in John Ward's late-Georgian Calverley New Town were situated at some distance from the market, shops, baths and library on The Pantiles. However, Decimus Burton's plan for the Calverley Estate included such facilities, so that residents could enjoy similar amenities to those living nearer the Wells.

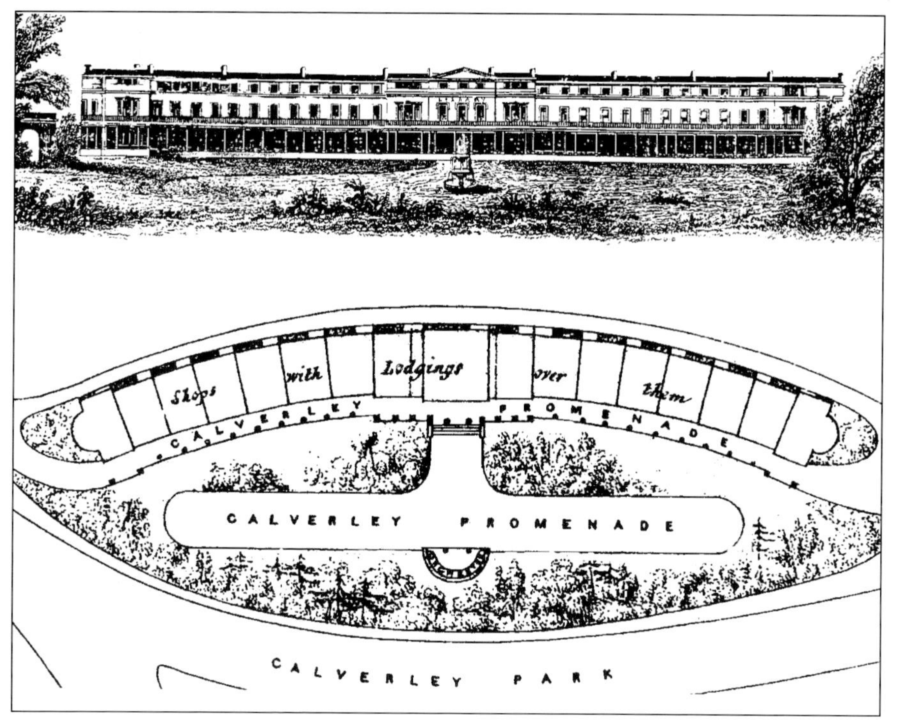

Calverley Park Crescent, formerly Calverley Promenade.

Originally called Calverley Promenade, Calverley Park Crescent was designed as a range of 17 shops, with residences over them. These faced south-east, looking over the Park and distant scenery, rendered them, it was thought, "highly eligible for lodgings".(5)

In front of the shops, a colonnade facing the Park, with light iron columns, opened at each end onto the roadway behind, which was at a lower level. In front of the Crescent, a large pleasure ground was attached to the centre of the range, where the respectable and fashionable company was allowed to promenade. The present carriageway between the colonnade and the pleasure garden was inserted at around the middle of the 19th. century (6) but, happily, a suggestion that the garden be split into 17 separate parcels has been resisted.

John Britton's account of Tunbridge Wells of 1832 shows Calverley Promenade to be 'proposed' at that time but, since several of the shops were trading by 1834, they must have been built around 1833. Plans could be viewed at Messrs. Bramah's premises in Calverley Road.

Advertisements of the period provide some interesting insights into activities in the Crescent during its early years.

ROYAL BATHS,

1, *Calverley Promenade,*

TUNBRIDGE WELLS.

Under the immediate Patronage of their Royal Highnesses

The Duchess of Kent,

AND

The Princess Victoria.

Mr. SEAMAN, Proprietor of the Royal Baths, No. 9, Suffolk Place, Pall-Mall East, London, at the request of the Nobility, Gentry, and faculty of this place and neighbourhood, has opened a branch Establishment at Calverley Promenade, on the same principles as pursued in the original Establishment of B. DOMINICETTI, M. D. who first introduced the system of Shampooing and Vapour Bathing into this Kingdom, in the year 1755, which is much improved by Mr. SEAMAN's experience in INDIA, enabling him to unite the advantages of the Indian and Turkish methods of Vapour Bathing and Shampooing.

Shampooing, Medicated Vapour, Aromatic, Sulphur, Barege, Nitro-Muriatic-Acid, Tepid, Douche, and Shower Baths.

At No.1, the Royal Baths offered Turkish and Indian bathing (perhaps of interest to East India Company employees who had retired to Tunbridge Wells) along with shampooing, medicated vapour, aromatic, sulphur, barege, Nitro-Muriatic acid, tepid, douch and shower baths.(7) Vapour baths seem generally to have been fed by fumes of gums, balsams and minerals, essences being absorbed through open pores into muscular and nervous fibres. Today only the extra chimney breast on the curved end bay serves as a reminder of the intriguing past of this particular house.

H. J. PETTIT,

(From London,)

Respectfully announces to the Nobility, Visitors, Residents, and Inhabitants generally, of Tunbridge Wells and its Vicinity, that he will open on WEDNESDAY, the 9th Instant, a Repository for the Sale of Miscellaneous Fancy Articles, in

Bronze & China Ornaments,

selected with great care from the first Houses in London, which he intends offering at such Prices as he trusts will meet general approbation.

H. J. P. will likewise have a select and fashionable Assortment of

Tunbridge Ware,

of every variety, and of the best workmanship; which he flatters himself will give satisfaction to those who may honour him by visiting his Establishment, at **No. 2,**

Adjoining the Baths, on the New Promenade.

Next door at No.2, a "select and fashionable assortment" of Tunbridge Ware was available, together with fancy goods, including bronze and china ornaments.

At No.7, the Royal Victoria Bazaar included among its merchandise white Windsor shaving cakes, Ferarie's German Eau de Cologne, orange tree toothpicks, button hooks, hair pins and patent teeth.

Beneath a central pediment at No. 9, the Royal Calverley Library sold Bibles, Books of Common Prayer, and fashionable vocal and instrumental music, as well as having globes, pianos and music available for hire. An annual subscription of £1-11s.-6d ($1\frac{1}{2}$ guineas) enabled perusal of newspapers, magazines, reviews and Army and Navy Lists in the Reading Room, together with works from the Library.

ROYAL

Calverley Library

AND

READING ROOM,

CALVERLEY PROMENADE,

TUNBRIDGE WELLS.

THE READING ROOM,

Is spacious, and well supplied with Magazines, Reviews, Army and Navy Lists, &c.

THE LIBRARY

Contains a good selection of the latest Publications on History, Biography, Voyages, Travels, Poetry, Novels, and Miscellaneous Literature; to which are added the most admired modern productions, as soon as published.

At No.13, a tailor Mr. Davis could "supply Gentlemen studying economy in dress" with "the first style of fashion" for ready money, while Mrs. Davis supplied "every article in the millinery and dress business upon te same reasonable terms".

MR. W. KING,

Surveyor, Auctioneer,

House & Estate Agent,

17, CALVERLEY PROMENADE,

Begs respectfully to announce that he has at present to dispose of or let for occupation, several capital detached Family VILLA RESIDENCES, furnished or unfurnished, situate in CALVERLEY PARK, the most beautiful part of this delightful Watering-place. They are adapted to the convenience and comfort of all classes of respectable families, and in addition to the advantages of scenery and external beauty of situation, which are rarely to be equalled, they are abundantly supplied with water from the celebrated Jack's Wood Spring.

The want of substantially-built and well-finished houses for families of respectability has hitherto been considerably felt at TUNBRIDGE WELLS; Mr. KING can, however, venture to state that the Villas now offered will be found to contain in every respect the abovementioned requisites.

Mr. KING has also to let several capital Houses with spacious Shops situate on the new Promenade, replete with every convenience and well adapted for any line of business.

Any communication made to Mr. KING, addressed as above will receive immediate attention.

9th May, 1835.

Estate Agent Mr. King at No.17 had available several of the "capital detached family villa residences in Calverley Park" which he described as "the most beautiful part of this delightful watering place."

Interestingly enough, Burton's original plan envisaged three more villas where Calverley Park Crescent now stands, and the decision instead to build shops and lodgings on that site, seems to have been taken after 1829. Perhaps in use terms, the original residential proposal was the right one for, by the 1840s, most of the shops had been converted to residential use. Thus, by the time Bagshaw's Directory was published in 1847, only Sarah Thomas's Baths and Edwin Marks' Library remained in commercial hands.

What does survive, however, is the "handsome appearance" of the promenade and its aspect overlooking the beauty of Calverley Park.

CHAPTER 3

NEVILL PARK AND HUNGERSHALL PARK

BY GEOFFREY AND BRENDA COPUS

The aristocratic families who had long been landowners in the area were not far behind in following the example of the newcomer John Ward, with his development of the Calverley Park estate and the "new town" of Tunbridge Wells. The Nevills, Earls and later Marquesses of Abergavenny, owned great estates in Kent and Sussex, including considerable tracts of land which were gradually developed as residential areas of Tunbridge Wells. Among these was Hungershall Farm and over 120 acres in Rusthall, then in the parish of Speldhurst – it had been owned by the Nevills for many generations, and was held of the Manor of Rusthall (described as Hungershall Walk) by an annual quit-rent of 10s.4d. This was an attractive site for expensive, "genteel" houses, adjoining the Common to the east, with a fine outlook over a steeply sloping valley. The northern side was to be developed first, as Nevill Park, and the ridge on the other side was later to be built up in similar style, as Hungershall Park, covenants being placed on the fields between the two, which were to remain open for ever.

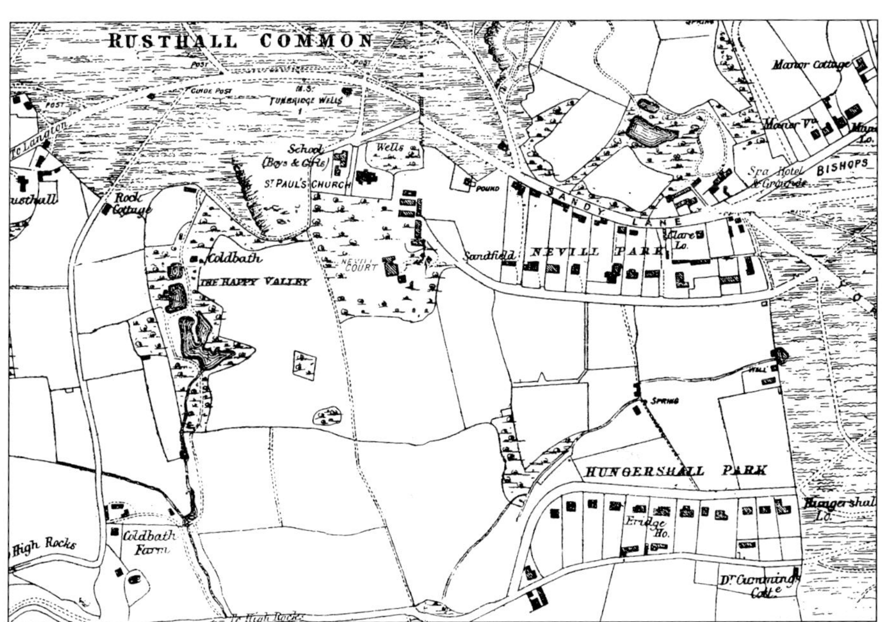

Nevill and Hungershall Parks, with Nevill Court and Happy Valley.

By an agreement of 1831 James Richardson, a Tunbridge Wells builder, was granted a lease of part of the land, which apart from building plots included the old White Hart and other existing houses on the Langton Road, some of which have survived to this day. Under the terms of the lease Richardson agreed to build at least three "good and substantial messuages or dwelling houses" at a minimum cost of £3,000. The Earl of Abergavenny, who granted the lease, undertook on his part to make a road at his own expense, to serve the houses planned for the new estate, and also to erect lodges at each entrance "with proper gates thereto". The road runs from Major York's Road to a point east of the present St. Paul's Church, with lodges on the edge of the Common at each end.

Stidolph's map of 1838 shows that by then the first houses had already been built – they were the pair Nos. 1 and 2, No. 3 and No. 6. These and the lodges are still the only houses shown in Nevill Park on the Speldhurst Tithe Map of 1840. Colbran's Tunbridge Wells Guide of the same date mentions Decimus Burton as the developer of Nevill Park. Certainly the first houses to be built are not unlike those designed by Burton at about the same time for Calverley Park, although no further evidence as to his involvement has yet been found. The two little lodges have fretted bargeboards, and No. 3, called "The Priory", has a suitably picturesque air. The name of the well-known architect George Basevi (who died in 1845) has been tentatively associated with No. 6. While this has not been confirmed it is interesting that Nathaniel Basevi of Lincoln's Inn (presumably George's brother of this name) was mentioned in a lease of another Nevill Park property, now called Ayot House, dated 1863.

Nevill Park.

A detailed survey of the Nevill Estates, made in 1899, is at East Sussex Record Office, and from the dates of the leases it would appear that the remainder of the original houses were built between 1847 and 1863. The survey gives the information that Nevill Park is a private road "but the Marquess has a key of the gates. The Lodge Keeper is selected by the owners of the several houses, but the Lodge Gate is held direct from the Marquess at a rent of £15 per annum, the custodian of the Park (at present Messrs. Stone and Simpson) collecting the rent and paying the same over to the Estate…" The development seems to have been a successful enterprise from the start, and a study of the 1901 Census returns confirms the generous scale on which the houses were run. As a typical example, Elizabeth Morton, a widow of 88 living at No. 5, had two Companions, a sick nurse, cook, parlourmaid and housemaid. Other establishments such as Estcourt had coachmen and their families living in stable blocks.

Nevill Court, c.1900.

The nineteenth century development comprised the two houses called Estcourt and Stoneleigh and Nos. 1-10 along the north of the estate road, completed with the building of No. 11 which took up the whole of the site on the slopes at the western end of the valley. Here was built Nevill Court, a mansion large even by Victorian standards, in an Italianate style, with a tower somewhat reminiscent of Queen Victoria's own beloved Osborne. It stood in some 50 acres of park-land, with its own lodge, but by 1930 it was seen as a white elephant, while the grounds were tempting to developers looking to complete Nevill Park in the spirit of the original intentions. With this in mind the house was demolished, although extensive retaining walls, the lodge and a stable block have survived.

A plan of the proposed new estate from 1930 naturally emphasises the "open fields which cannot be built upon" and also marks Happy Valley to the west as "preserved for ever as an open space." Two roads are shown leading onto High Rocks Lane to the south, but in fact there has only ever been footpath access from that side. It would seem that

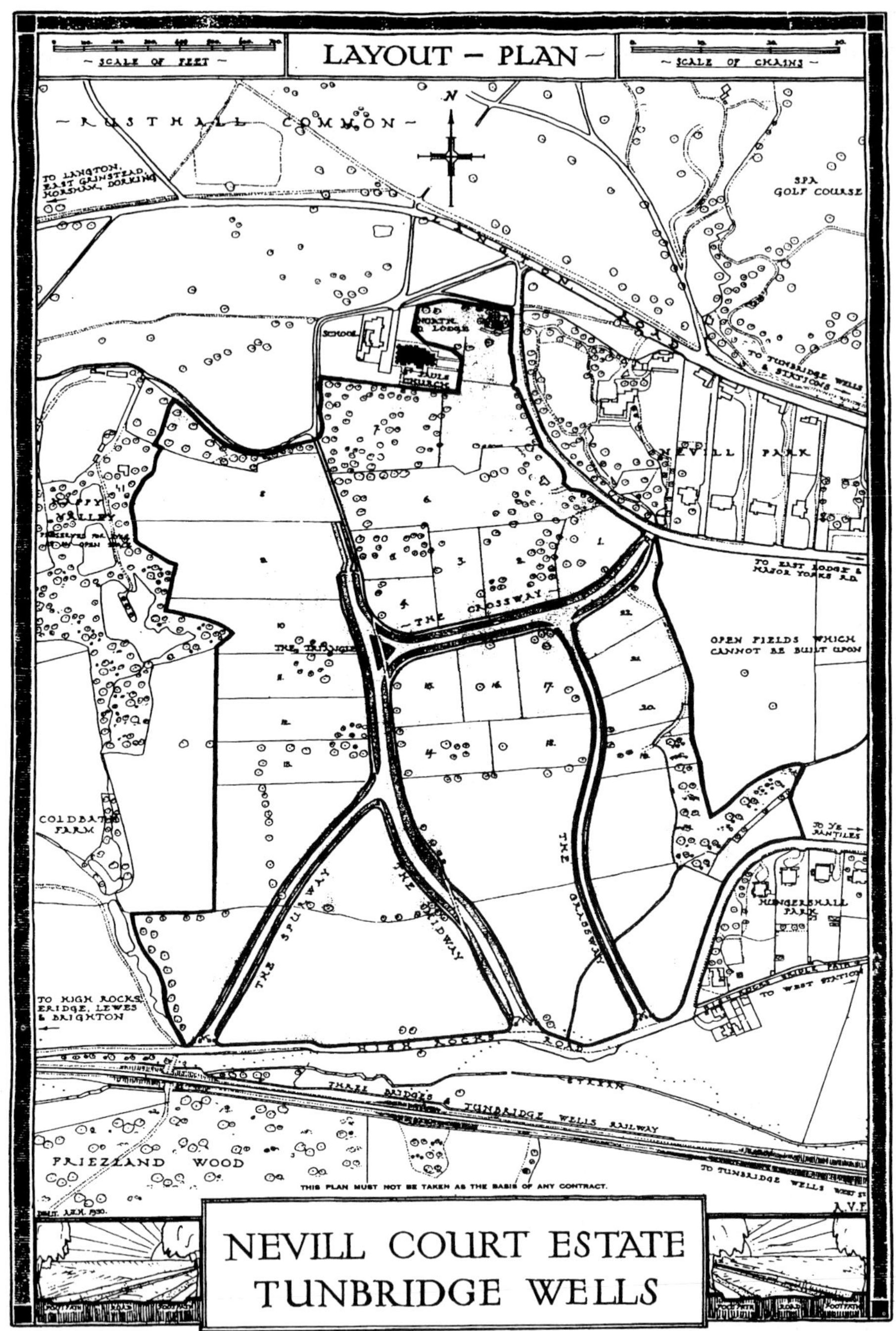
LAYOUT – PLAN
SCALE OF FEET
SCALE OF CHAINS
N
RUSTHALL COMMON
TO LANGTON, EAST GRINSTEAD, HORSHAM, DORKING
SPA GOLF COURSE
SCHOOL
NORTH LODGE
ST PAULS CHURCH
TO TUNBRIDGE WELLS & STATIONS
NEVILL PARK
TO EAST LODGE & MAJOR YORKS RD.
THE CROSSWAY
THE TRIANGLE
OPEN FIELDS WHICH CANNOT BE BUILT UPON
COLDBATH FARM
TO YE PANTILES
THE SPUR WAY
THE RIDWAY
THE GREENWAY
HUNGERSHALL PARK
TO WEST STATION
TO HIGH ROCKS, ERIDGE, LEWES & BRIGHTON
HIGH ROCKS ROAD
STREAM
THREE BRIDGES & TUNBRIDGE WELLS RAILWAY
FRIEZLAND WOOD
THIS PLAN MUST NOT BE TAKEN AS THE BASIS OF ANY CONTRACT.
TO TUNBRIDGE WELLS WEST ST.
NEVILL COURT ESTATE
TUNBRIDGE WELLS

Plan of 1930.

Frank Baird, who clung tenaciously to every possible right to be claimed in his position as Lord of the Manor of Rusthall, made difficulties about crossing what he asserted was Manorial waste.

In a letter of 31 October 1930 preserved in the Manorial archives, Mr. Baird's agents told him that Mr. Bennett, the developer, had said that "he must first be convinced that there was in fact existing waste of the Manor over which it would be necessary for his roads to pass... he said he would be willing to pay £5, to this we refused to listen ... We pointed out to him that if proceedings resulted he was bound to incur very considerable expense whatever the result, but he expressed himself as quite prepared to face this consequence..." It would seem that in the event wiser counsels prevailed and the developer dropped the idea of roads to the south, which in the long run has had a beneficial effect. This part of the Nevill Park estate, known collectively as Nevill Court, has gradually been built up over many years from the thirties up to the present time, the houses standing in large gardens with well-established trees and shrubs, and with extensive views over Kent and Sussex.

The evident success of the Nevill Park enterprise led to a similar development along the southern side of the "land not to be built upon", where the mansions of Hungershall Park were built between 1854 and 1867. Terence Davies, writing in 1976 in his thoughtful study "Tunbridge Wells. The Gentle Aspect" describes the houses as "of a wayward and eccentric, perhaps sinister appearance, in styles difficult to define and nearly all determined to be highly individual." These comments may now appear rather harsh, with changing tastes enabling us to appreciate more the eclectic nature of much Victorian architecture.

Henry Hickman Cronk.

The only architect known to be associated with the development is the local Henry Hickman Cronk. He is mentioned by John Newman in the West Kent "Buildings of England" volume as having designed No. 11 in 1862, the house costing £2,132 to build. Sale particulars of No. 3 when it came on the market in 1890 give an excellent description of this typical house, revealing that although there were three large bedrooms and two dressing rooms on the first floor, and five "good secondary and servants' bedrooms" there was not one bathroom in the house. Evidently this was felt as a disadvantage even by that date, particulars say that one of the dressing rooms "could be easily converted into a Bath Room." The grounds comprised nearly two acres, including a detached block of stabling with "a coach house, harness room and three rooms over for Coachman, capital four roomed cottage for Gardener, – there is a well-drained Meadow adjoining the second kitchen garden, about 3 acres 3 roods 36 perches in extent..."

A study of the Census returns of both Parks in 1871 gives a fascinating insight into the type of people who had come to settle there. Not one of the heads of household had been born in Tunbridge Wells or anywhere near. In Nevill Park, for instance, six had been born in London, and one each in Ireland, Scotland and Nottinghamshire. There were four Anglican clergy, including at 9 Nevill Park, Walter Trower, "late Bishop of Gibraltar, now sub-dean of Exeter." Other occupations included Medical Doctor, not practising; barrister, not practising; annuitant; retired woolbroker; Lieutenant General (born Nova Scotia) and sugar refiner (born Russia, British subject).

In the 1861 Census, Charles Richardson of 10 Nevill Park describes himself as "a proprietor of houses" and admits that he was born in Shoreditch, but by 1871 he has come round to being "retired from business" and just gives London as his birthplace. No doubt he and other self-made men who had settled here were anxious to establish themselves in a new environment and in an atmosphere of gentility. Time must have passed very slowly for these families, particularly for the considerable number of spinsters. Twenty households were present when the 1871 Census was taken, making up a total of 64 "genteel" inhabitants, and they had 101 servants, including 13 dependants, to look after their needs.

One redoubtable inhabitant, who lived first at 3 Hungershall Park and later at Estcourt, Nevill Park, was John Stone Wigg, a great philantrophist who became the first Mayor of Tunbridge Wells in 1889. He was in constant correspondence with the Nevill Estate Office regarding the state of Hungershall Park road and whether the Town Commissioners could or should repair it. Other topics which occur in estate correspondence include a proposal by a builder in 1903 to erect ten houses on the open land, the enquirer being referred politely to the Nevills' Warwick Park estate as a possible alternative. An early suggestion by Strange and Sons that an overhead electric cable might be put in across the valley also provoked a strong adverse reaction.

In 1926 the agent for Lord Abergavenny, "in accordance with the Rusthall Manor Acts 1863 and 1902", put in a claim for him to be recognised as "a freehold tenant of the Manor as being tenant in tail male in possession". The attached particulars list in great detail all the houses in Nevill Park and Hungershall Park, and also the Beacon and nearby properties. The total rents received from Nevill Park were £3,882 (of which Miss Cohen of Nevill Court paid £638) and from Hungershall Park £2,645. Such was the tenacity of the Lord of the Manor of Rusthall that he raised the question of demanding the payment of a Heriot – the best live beast belonging to the Manorial tenant – when the Marquess died in the following year.

Attempts to nibble away at the essentially rural environment of the twin parks have continued up to the present day. It is encouraging that, so far, all have been successfully resisted because of the original Covenants on the open fields. Generally speaking, any new buildings have fitted in well with the principles established in such different circumstances over 170 years ago.

Hungershall Park c. 1870.

CHAPTER 4

CAMDEN PARK

by Geoffrey and Brenda Copus

George Charles Pratt, 2nd. Marquess Camden, (1799-1866) was possessed of very large estates in Kent, and also in Wales, London and Middlesex. The Kent estate was centred on Bayham Abbey and included a substantial part of Tunbridge Wells.

The successful development of the Calverley Estate by John Ward of Holwood turned the thoughts of other local landowners towards the potential profit to be made from similar schemes, and no doubt the arrival of the railway in 1844 accelerated the process.

In the Tunbridge Wells area, Lord Abergavenny and Lord Camden were the undisputed leaders of society, and both laid out estates on the

Camden Park, c.1865.

Calverley Park lines – the former at Nevill Park and later at Hungershall Park; and the latter at Camden Park.

The description of Lord Camden's intentions given in Colbran's handbook and directory of 1847 can hardly be bettered- "There is some building land recently laid out by the Marquess Camden, in plots of one acre each, for the erection of a number of first-class residences....the land is...admirably chosen for the purpose, having the advantage of a private park, and yet within an easy walk of the mineral springs and the business part of the town..."

The first evidence of the development appears in covenants drafted in 1846; these chiefly refer to the type of building to be erected and to the planting to be carried out; only evergreens and shrubs, not forest trees, were to be planted in the gardens, and no building was to be erected or altered without the approval of the Marquess Camden. The final version of the covenants added that no dwelling house of less value than £1200 was to be erected, and only one house in each of the plots of about one acre. No school, trade, business or manufacture was to be carried on. For his part, the Marquess undertook that he and his successors would always keep the 7½ acres of open land in the middle of the estate as meadow or pasture land.

By the time of the 1851 Census, only the east and west lodges had been built, but it is useful in dating the commencement of the development because it lists "two new houses building".

No. 1 Camden Park.

No. 1, Camden Park, known as Salesmere, is one of a group of five built during the first years of the development; it has a tower and a fine contemporary conservatory. When it was up for sale in 1898 the particulars described it as in "the Italianate style" and say that it was built "for a former Marquess Camden for the occupation of his sister." Be that as it may, it seems likely that it was one of the two "new houses building" mentioned in the 1851 Census, since the property was conveyed by Lord Camden to the Misses Eliza and Henrietta Terry in 1856. Bearing in mind the statement in the lawsuit of 1887 mentioned below that plots were sold from 1856 onwards, it is probable that this is the earliest house in the Park, although the other four in the group (Nos. 2 to 5) must date from about the same time.

Who was the architect responsible for this first stage in the development, it is not possible to say with complete certainty. Colbran in 1847 speaks of D. Burton, Esq. as the architect for the estate, but there is no evidence that he was in fact involved when building eventually started. William Willicombe's obituary in the Kent and Sussex Courier (1875) gives a long list of his works and mentions among them houses in Camden Park. This is confirmed by documents among the Camden papers, including a very detailed specification by Willicombe for a house to be built at "plot 2", dated 30 August 1862. Unfortunately, there are no plans with this, or with a specification for the erection of an entrance lodge, of the same date. An accompanying letter offers to erect the house for £2,730 and two lodges, similar to each other, for £550. Careful study of the various plans of the estate leads to the conclusion that plot 2 was the site of No. 5, Camden Park – the house now known as The Lawn. This was purchased in 1863 by General Sir John Fowler Bradford (and subsequently lived in by W.C.Cripps, the first Town Clerk of Tunbridge Wells), so presumably the house was erected in about that year; it is Italianate and stuccoed and very similar in character to others by Willicombe elsewhere in the town. Nos. 2 and 4 are also stuccoed, but No. 3 is of stone, with an impressive inset porch with Tuscan columns. On balance, it seems likely that all are by Willicombe; his firm of Willicombe and Oakley were certainly responsible for the drainage system, a source of some difficulties from time to time in the early period.

Here, even more perhaps than in Calverley Park, the residents of the houses grouped round the meadow all have the illusion that they are gazing out over their own ancestral acres.

It is interesting to see from the 1871 Census who was living there at the time. General Bradford, mentioned above, was undoubtedly the lion of the Park: although aged 66 he was described as "Lt. General in HM Indian Army, Active List". At No. 4 lived George Ware, a solicitor, with his sister; the head of the household of No. 3 was away at the time and his daughter, Harriett Rogers, aged 16, was presiding over 7 servants. At No. 2, Thomas Duckworth Headlam frankly gave his profession as "living on interest of money", while at No. 1 the Misses

Terry, who also had a butler, lady's maid, housemaid, cook and gardener in residence, indicated no occupation at all. Life must have passed very quietly in these surroundings at that period...

However the development of the Park had been somewhat slow, if not disappointing to its owner, the Marquess, and family circumstances were to bring pressure on its future.

The second Marquess Camden had married Harriett, daughter of George Murray, Bishop of Rochester; the Marriage Settlement of 1835 is a large and impressive document on such thick parchment that it is difficult even to open. There were three sons and eight daughters of this marriage. When the 2nd. Marquess died in 1866, the detailed return for probate purposes shows that the Camden estates had an annual value of £19,817-2s.-4d, but under his will the estate was charged with the payment of annuities of £200 and Jointures of £2000 to each of the eight daughters; also £7000 to each of the younger sons at 21 (less £3000 already paid to the elder of these.)

This must have represented something of a drain even on the resources of the estate, but nevertheless the eldest son, John Charles, third Marquess Camden, set about building a very ambitious new seat at Bayham. In the midst of this, he died at the age of 32, in 1872, leaving a daughter and an only surviving son, also called John Charles, fourth Marquess Camden, who was only a few months old. The management of the Estate passed effectively to Trustees and Agents.

The correspondence in the Camden papers of this period refers to a deed "directed by the Court of Chancery to be indorsed upon the Bayham settlement" and it is evident that this was intended to ensure the payment of the bequests in the will of the third Marquess. The Tunbridge Wells property formed part of the Bayham estate and it became a matter of some urgency to dispose of the rest of the Camden Park plots, and attempts to do this at this period are well-documented.

A letter of 1874 from the Camdens' London solicitors to J D Cramer Roberts, the agent of the Bayham estate, who lived at Frant, says "it will be a great relief to all parties to have their portions raised and paid – if Lady Camden (i.e. the Dowager Marchioness) is at Bayham you can consult her as well as Messrs Stone. Pray turn over in your mind what portions may advantageously be advertised and offered..."

Cramer Roberts, in a letter of the same year, comments that the land ought to sell for £450 to £500 an acre, but adds pessimistically "there is something about Camden Park the public do not fancy. I see house building every day on sites which to my mind are not nearly so pretty nor advantageous but we seldom have any enquiries for land at Camden Park. I am certain you ought not to press a Sale if it can be avoided, as all the land near the Station will soon be sold and they must come to us in the end..."

However, the London solicitors were inclined to take the opposite view, and thought that "any probable increase in the value of that land will not compensate for the loss involved in the large amount of interest rolling up against the inheritance on account of the payments to the younger children..." and Cramer Roberts came round to the view that the remaining Camden Park lots should be put up to auction.

Early in 1875 there was a diversion, Frank Stone the local solicitor writing to say that he had had an offer of 10,000 guineas for 20 acres of the estate; Stone's opinion was that the offer should be accepted. Cramer Roberts agreed, saying that "there is now a large quantity of property for sale in and around Tunbridge Wells, for which there is apparently much difficulty in finding purchasers". In the end however the prospective purchaser became "very unreasonable" and withdrew, the solicitors commenting that "looking to his temper I do not regret that it is off." The auction was eventually authorised by the trustees and took place on 13 August 1875, but the results were very disappointing – there were few bidders or bids and only three lots were sold, the proceeds coming to £3,650.

A detailed map of about 1883 shows the subsequent history of the disposal of much of the estate, as well as nearby land at Hawkenbury which was also Camden property. From this it appears that seven plots were bought about this time by Mr Castle – these were adjacent sites on Bayhall Road as far as the northern entrance to Camden Park and were part of the Camden Park estate. Frederick James Castle, described in the local paper in 1887 as "a well-known land agent", would nowadays be called a developer. He was responsible for laying out many of the less exclusive areas of the town and so his appearance in Camden Park is somewhat surprising. A newspaper report of 10 June 1887 reveals what his motives were, carrying a fascinating account of a case where he was the defendant in an action brought by Brenton Halliburton Collins and Mrs Stoddart Douglass. Collins was a formidable opponent, being the owner of Dunorlan and much surrounding land, and Mrs Douglass of Chilston House had purchased Halls Hole Farm from the Camden estate in 1883. The report tells how the Marquess Camden had tried to sell plots in Camden Park (incidentally giving 1856 as the date when sales commenced) with covenants to ensure that no house would be built at a cost of under £1,200. However, not all the plots had sold and the defendant had bought up a number of them and had tried to purchase the remainder with a view to erecting house which would cost only £600 each; it is interesting, incidentally, that as early as 1869, Stone had written to Cramer Roberts, warning him that they suspected Castle had it in mind to do this.

The Court heard expert evidence from Henry Hickman Cronk the architect, to the effect that reducing the class of houses in this way would damage the character of the surrounding property, and issued an injunction restraining Mr Castle from doing this, costs being granted to the plaintiffs. The houses later built on these plots were certainly substantial enough to satisfy the most critical local resident, worried about falling property values.

Originally, Oakfield Court stood in its own grounds stretching down to Prospect Road, but these were built on earlier in this century. Colbran, quoted above, speaks of "excellent residences in the neighbourhood, among the most recently built (being) Oak Field Court, a beautiful stone-faced mansion belonging to Demetrius Grevis James Esq..." The design compares to those of the Calverley Park villas and it seems at least possible that it, too, was designed by Burton. The metal canopy, a typical Burton motif, has unfortunately disappeared, leaving only its outline behind.

In Bayhall Road, there are more extremely substantial houses, in large mature gardens. The architecture owes something to Norman Shaw and the revival' of interest in English domestic buildings of earlier centuries. The view they enjoy at present is an outstanding one, over the rolling, tree-dotted landscape of the Dunorlan estate, and here again we find cows grazing; there cannot be many towns the size of Tunbridge Wells which have so many rural areas within a short distance of the urban centre.

Camster.

If one enters Camden Park by the northern lodge, there is on the left the fine view of Camster, which has a long drive and lawn leading to it. Camster, set well back behind a. light screen of trees, looks like an illustration by

Randolph Caldecott. Designed in the Wren tradition, it was built for Mrs Strong in 1905 and is the earliest known work by the eminent local architect, Cecil Burns.

Burns was born in 1882 and went to Tonbridge School. He then worked in the office of Sir Reginald Blomfield before setting up in practice on his own account in Tunbridge Wells, which he continued for some 60 years: he died in 1969. His buildings include the neo-Georgian Tunbridge Wells and Counties Club (1909), Eynsham House, St John's Road (now the offices of the Freight Transport Association, but built as a Christian Science Church, 1931), the Kent and Sussex Hospital (1934). In 1945 he contributed largely to a report published by the Civic Association, suggesting future plans for the town. In 1959 he was a founder member of the "59" Society, forerunner of the Civic Society.

No. 6 Camden Park.

Continuing past Camster, we pass several other large detached houses dating from the turn of the century and then there is the house which was formerly St Peter's Vicarage (No.6), now divided into two and known as Holly House and West House. Obviously it is by an architect of no ordinary ability; built of red brick, with tile hanging to the first floor, it has a most impressive roof, with two sets of dormer windows. The chimney stacks are very substantial, and the whole is reminiscent of the work of Norman Shaw.

In fact, the architect was Ewan Christian (1814-95) who is generally thought of in connection with churches rather than domestic buildings. However, his position as architect to the Ecclesiastical Commissioners from 1850 meant that he had oversight of the many new vicarages and rectories which Victorian piety and enthusiasm produced. In most instances he acted as an advisor but on occasion, as here, he was his own architect. In the immediate area, he was architect of St James', Tunbridge Wells, and Hildenborough Church, further afield, and in another style, Christian was the architect of the National Portrait Gallery in Trafalgar Square. He was President of the Royal Institute of British Architects, 1884-6, and Royal Gold Medallist.

CHAPTER 5

BISHOP'S DOWN PARK, MOLYNEUX PARK AND BOYNE PARK

by Geoffrey and Brenda Copus

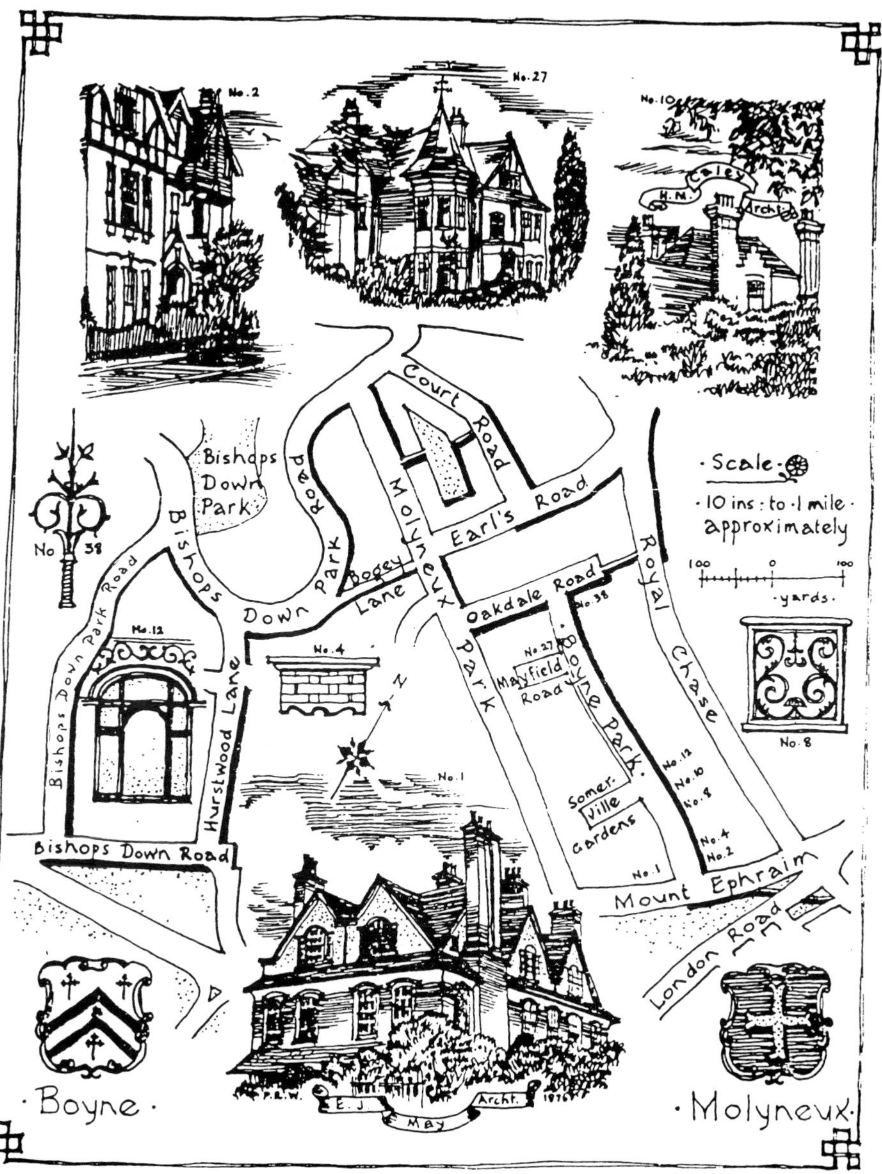

From the mid-17th. century onwards, residences and superior lodging houses began to be built along Mount Ephraim, which is the highest point in the area and overlooks the Common and Town of Tunbridge Wells. This development continued to spread slowly with the building of a fringe of substantial mansions along the ridge, some standing in their own extensive park-like grounds, but behind these the country remained open until well into the 19th. century.

Thomas Montagu Martin Weller, Lieutenant Colonel in the West Kent Militia, was Lord of the Manor of Rusthall from 1853 until his death in 1888, although he lived at Kingsgate in Rolvenden. Following the fashionable and evidently lucrative trend for landowners to develop residential parks in and near Tunbridge Wells, he promoted an ambitious scheme on his land some way from the town. This was situated down the slope behind the fringe of houses along Bishop's Down, approached by Hurstwood Lane, which was extended with a private road encircling an area of several acres, on which a lake had been formed.

The first sale of building plots would appear to have been in 1864, when 9 lots were put up for auction, and 3 were sold. In August 1865 a further 31 lots were auctioned. The auctioneers wrote that "the Park has been planned and laid out with the greatest taste and judgment; the variety and extent of the Timber thereon forms a feature of much beauty; and the Property generally is admirably adapted for the erection of First-class Villa Residences, for which in this particular locality there has been, for some time past, a great demand... The Vendor intends to maintain the land marked on the Plan as "not to be built on", containing about five acres, always as Pasture Land only, and the several purchasers will have the privilege of using such land at all times for purposes of recreation." Typical of the period, the Covenants placed on the properties specifically exclude servants from boating or fishing in the lake.

The claims made for the property were not unreasonable, but despite this the Park never really developed as Col. Weller had hoped it would. An Indenture of 23 November 1865 records the sale of 21 of the plots to Sir David Lionel Salomons, and 7 plots to three other purchasers. Although a beautiful coloured plan, probably from 1864, shows in detail 9 houses with elaborately laid out gardens, this is a flight of fancy since only 3 of these were ever built. They were on adjacent plots at the southern end of the park, and only one of them, the house

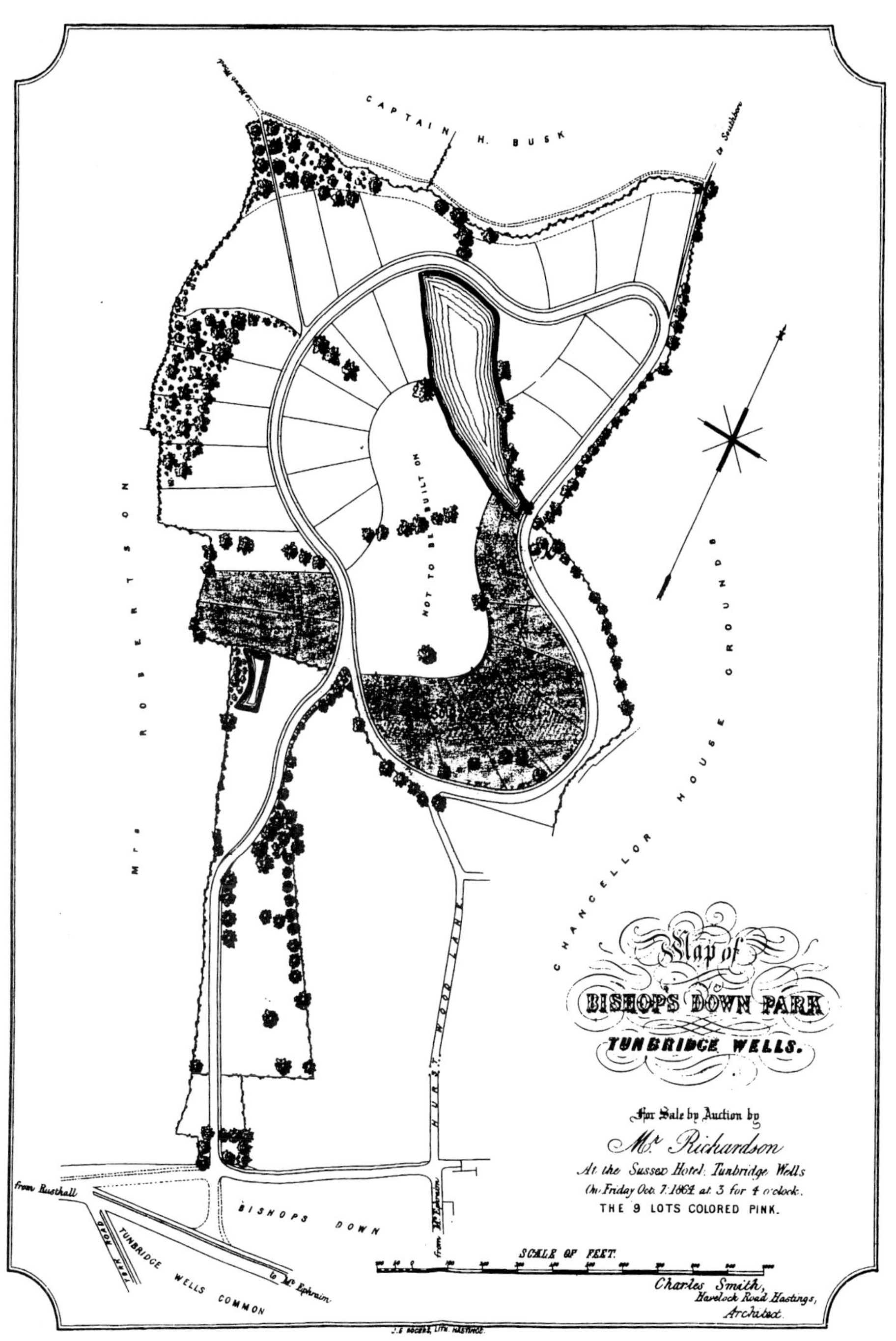

Bishop's Down Park 1864.

called Studley, which is known to have been designed by William Willicombe, has survived. These three, and a fourth house, originally called Lake House but soon renamed Warberry House, are all shown on the 25" OS map of 1867.

Warberry House was built over several plots, taking up all of the land on the north side of the lake, and sale particulars of 1886 show that it was a most elaborate building with a tower containing "an Observatory or Smoking Room...opening by a glazed door to a spacious Belvedere enclosed by balustrades." There were 17 bedrooms, the principal one measuring 26 feet by 18 feet, while on the ground floor the two drawing rooms had sliding doors between them so that they could be used together "forming a Noble Apartment, upwards of 40 ft. in length."

There was "capital modern stabling ... at a convenient distance from the Residence" while in the "prettily timbered and shrubbed grounds" were two tennis lawns and a fives' court. This huge building, unsuited to modern requirements, fell on hard times and was demolished, and in recent years the valuable site was fought over with numerous planning applications before the present blocks of apartments were built.

Bishop's Down Park remained very much of a backwater for many years, and it was not until the period between the two World Wars that building began again. The OS maps show that even by 1936 only twelve more houses had been built, while the land to the west of Bishop's Down Park Road had been incorporated into the Spa Golf Course. Since then the plots have gradually been built on, with houses which – while they are far removed in scale from the enormous Victorian mansions – well fulfil the intentions of the original developer. The "ground not to be built upon" with its mature trees and shrubs and its large lake may well claim to be the most beautiful among those maintained for the enjoyment of the inhabitants of the residential parks of Tunbridge Wells.

Although Bishop's Down Park proved an initial disappointment to its promoters, two other estates which were built from the nineties onwards, nearer to the increasingly prosperous town, were a good deal more successful.

Hon. F. G. Molyneux.

The Hon. F. G. Molyneux lived for many years at Earl's Court, one of the mansions built along Mount Ephraim, and his name occurs frequently in the local newspapers as one of the great and the good of Tunbridge Wells. When he died in 1886 the Kent and Sussex Courier was printed with a black border and carried a lengthy obituary, listing his many achievements in improving the developing town. It is perhaps ironic that the increasing popularity of Tunbridge Wells in late Victorian times led to the break-up of the Earl's Court estate, because Mr. Molyneux's heirs evidently decided that the time was ripe to cash in on the increasingly lucrative market.

What was to be called the Molyneux Park estate was laid out, with Molyneux Park Road being constructed on the site of an existing farm track, leading down the dip slope to the new Earl's Road and Court Road.

Following the example of other developments, the Molyneux Park Estate had its own private park, albeit quite a small one, which in a map attached to a Deed of 31 December 1900 is shown laid out as a "lawn tennis and recreation ground". The map shows the 99 numbered plots whose owners were entitled to the exclusive use of the park and the deed records the regulations applying to the recreation ground. Each householder was to subscribe one guinea a year, the use of bicycles on the grass was strictly forbidden and residents were expected to assist the Committee in preventing the use of the gardens as a thoroughfare by tradesmen.

Earl's Court itself and the grounds immediately behind it were not included in the estate. The house, of two storeys only, was greatly extended in 1904 by the local architects Henry Hickman Cronk and Egbert Cronk. Two further floors, a large extra wing and a prominent tower, in a flamboyant French chateau style, were added, and it became the Earl's Court Hotel. Some time after the Second World War it became home to the Reliance Insurance Group, but in a reversion to its original residential use it has recently been converted to 36 apartments, many of the original features, restored after a serious fire, being retained.

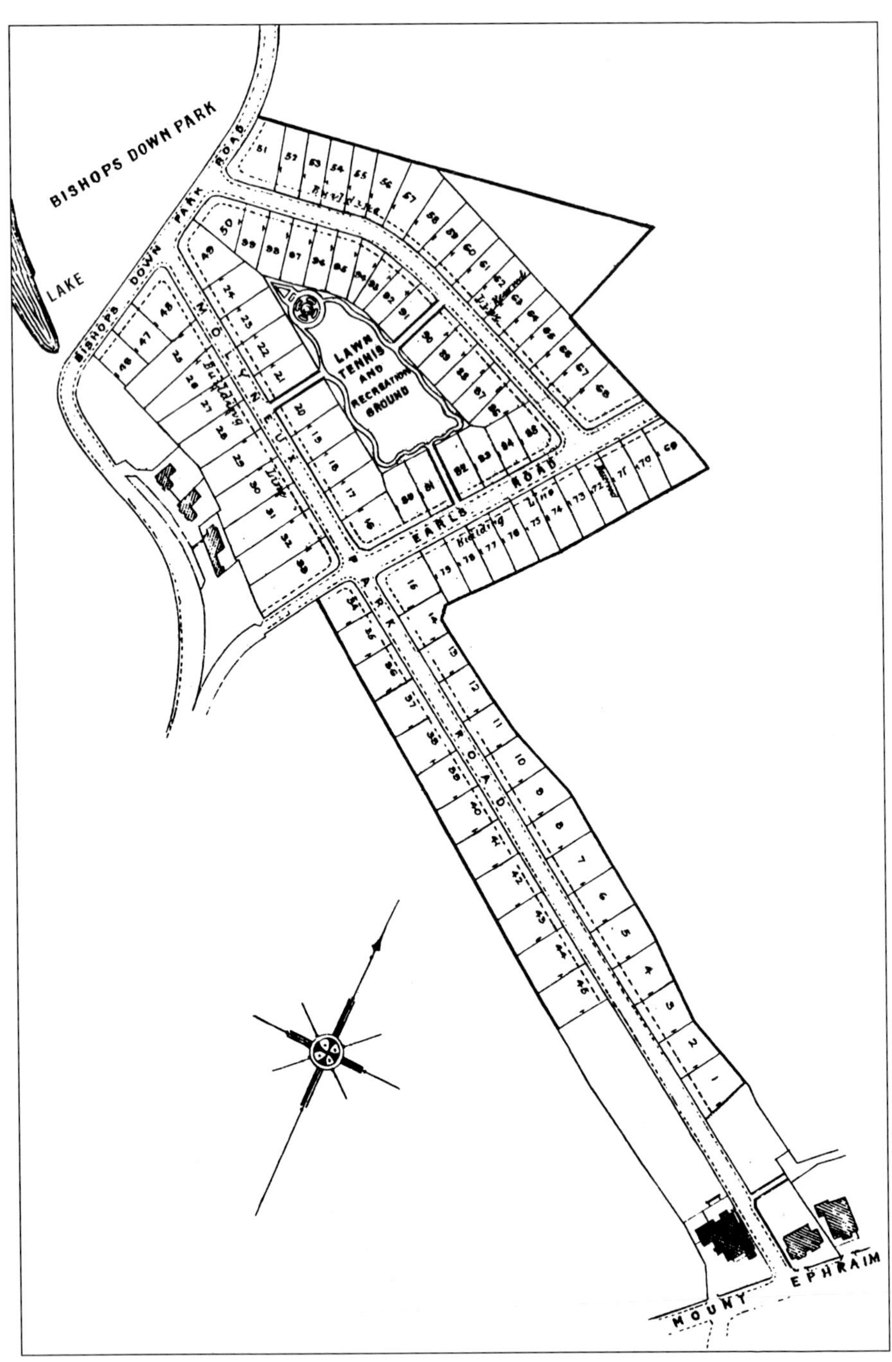

The Molyneux Park estate, 1891

Houses very soon began to be built on the new estate, the first planning application being for a detached house in Molyneux Park Road dated 10 October 1891, followed in June and July 1892 by applications for houses in Court Road and Earl's Road.

William Barnsley Hughes was the architect of most of the early houses; a typical Victorian entrepreneur, whose impact on the Tunbridge Wells scene was considerable, he had a rather chequered career. Perhaps his most endearing building is the Friendly Societies' Hall in Camden Road, sporting the attractive Camden elephants, while his most impressive work must be the huge stable block built for Sir David Salomons at Broomhill, Southborough. He was less successful as the developer of the Liptraps Estate based around Sandhurst Road. As Vera Coomber tactfully notes in her extensive research into Hughes, "financial pressures led him to emigrate to Canada with his wife and several children in 1910" where he became a much respected resident of Edmonton, Alberta.

The Rev. F. F. Walrond, Vicar of Rusthall, wrote in 1900 of his new parishioners in Molyneux Park that "they all of them belong to the comfortable class." A study of the Census returns of the following year confirms this view, and shows that by then there were some 60 inhabited houses on the estate. "Living on own means" is given as the occupation of 23 heads of households, while there are three medical men, two solicitors, a General of the Staff Corps and numbers of prosperous tradesmen. Less comfortable would have been the 124 servants on the estate, nearly every household having at least a cook and a housemaid living in. The only national figure living here at that time was the young E.M. Forster, whose parents had come to live at 10 Earl's Road when he was a pupil at Tonbridge School. He recorded his dislike both of the School and of Tunbridge Wells itself. In 1901 he was aged 22, living in a typical household with his widowed mother, his grandmother and a housemaid and cook.

For descriptions of the houses themselves the Valuation Office records – the so-called "New Domesday" survey of 1910-1915 – are invaluable. Every house was briefly surveyed and the details recorded include the names of owners and tenants, the value of the property and the rent paid – owner-occupiers were relatively rare. The surveyor who inspected Earl's Road mentions that there were a number of vacant properties, a situation which he ascribed to the distance from the town. Typical annual rents were £85 for a detached corner house and £47.10s.0d. for a semi-detached house in Court Road.

Hollin House.

A triangular site behind Court Road was not included in the original numbered plots, although a driveway to it was left vacant. In Edwardian times it was suggested as a suitable site for a Mission Church in connection with St. Paul's Rusthall, but in the event it was not bought for that purpose, and soon afterwards Hollin House was built on it. This is a delightful building designed by Charles Bowles of Staple Inn, and the "New Domesday" surveyor (who seems to have had a special interest in woodwork and joinery, which he often criticised in other properties) waxed lyrical over it, even adding a sketch of the building to his notes. He described it as "a house of exceptional character being designed as on old English homestead. The oak joinery is hand worked and the members are morticed and pegged. The stoves too are of Dutch bricks and tiles. In every way an unusual house..."

In general, the estate has survived remarkably intact, although it is unfortunate that the original brick pavements the length of Molyneux Park Road were removed before the district became part of a Conservation Area. Unusual features such as the elaborate timber porches in some Court Road houses remain. Although after the Second World War large Victorian houses were seen as white elephants and were often divided into flats, they have now become popular once again. One recent development which would have been unthinkable not so long ago has been the building of two large houses designed very much in the spirit of their turn of the century neighbours, on a double plot formerly occupied by a bungalow in Earl's Road. The recreation ground with its mature trees remains a peaceful oasis, much appreciated and used by the inhabitants of the estate in ways which would be approved by the original developers.

Following the evident success of the Molyneux Park estate, it became apparent that the development of the neighbouring Boyne Park and its grounds of over 13 acres could be a profitable venture. By 1891 the owners decided that they too would sell out, and in the sale particulars the "family mansion" was described rather extravagantly as "at one time a residence of Her Majesty the Queen" – who had indeed stayed there for short periods many years before. The property included pleasure gardens, kitchen gardens, outhouses and meadows, containing altogether about 17 acres, situated in "unquestionably the choicest position in this fashionable inland Watering Place."

The whole estate was purchased by Charles John Gallard, a Southborough builder who wasted no time on sentiment but demolished the old house and set about laying out his new estate, which naturally he called Boyne Park. He first had to surmount the problem faced by so many property owners in the area – the rights claimed by the Manor of Rusthall. Among the extensive archives of the Manor is a deed with a plan showing that, for the privilege of crossing the narrow strip of Common bordering Mount Ephraim, Mr. Gallard was charged an exorbitant £300.

The estate was laid out on "park" principles, although it lacked the communally-owned ground which was a distinctive feature of earlier developments. Mr. Gallard laid out a network of roads – Boyne Park Road (later known just as Boyne Park), Somerville Gardens, Mayfield Road and Oakdale Road – dividing the land into building lots and erecting the first houses in 1893. In 1895 many of the lots were auctioned on building leases and the estate was largely built up as we see it today by 1910. It certainly fulfilled the developer's intention of providing "good-class private residences" and the credit for the attractive and varied way in which the area was laid out must be given chiefly to one man, the local architect Herbert Murkin Caley.

Herbert Murkin Caley.

Caley was born in 1859, the son of Murkin Lawrence Caley, also a Tunbridge Wells architect, about whom little is known. The value of his personal estate was only £117.0s.6d. when his widow Ellen proved his will in December 1883. Herbert had been articled to his father, and took over his practice, and his financial circumstances must have improved considerably by his marriage to Mary Cranwell Mills of Rusthall. They lived for many years at Cranwell House, at Lower Green in Rusthall, a very substantial house (now demolished) which he designed himself.

Caley's career thereafter was one long success story. He became a local Councillor in 1900 and was Mayor of Tunbridge Wells in 1908-9, being made a Freeman of the Borough in 1935. He was a prominent nonconformist and lay preacher, belonging to St. John's Free Church (now St. Andrew's United Reformed Church) which he had also designed, his name appearing on one of the foundation stones as both deacon and architect. Like William Barnsley Hughes, he left his mark on the face of Tunbridge Wells, including business premises in the town, the Culverden Hall, St. John's Road for the Plymouth Brethren and the Marlborough (now the Summit) Hotel, Mount Ephraim. However, his private houses are his best work, and in Boyne Park he had a golden opportunity to cater for the substantial middle class who were the backbone of the town. Most of the earlier houses on the estate are known or thought to have been designed by him. They are, to say the least, varied in character, with traces of many styles from Gothic to Queen Anne.

Boyne Tower.

Mr. Gallard reserved a prime site, No. 12 Boyne Park, for himself, and Caley designed for him in 1895 the eccentric and aptly named Boyne Tower – the gabled tower itself rising to a height of some fifty feet. The facade has an unusual broad frieze of decorative plasterwork with gilded mythical beasts which have an Elizabethan feeling. The huge chimney stacks on Caley's houses are a striking feature, while two of the corner houses, 27 and 38 Boyne Park, have turrets with spires, which break up the skyline in the way the Victorians loved. Stained glass features in the landing windows of some of the houses, surviving notably at 33 and 36 Boyne Park and 11a Oakdale Road.

Under the estate covenants, all the houses were to be detached, although in the event, a few semi-detached pairs were built. The houses in Boyne Park Road had to cost not less than £900, and those in Oakdale Road not less than £700 in materials and labour. Those fortunate to live in buildings designed by Caley, and built by Gallard, will testify to their wonderfully solid qualities.

Having said this, the single most attractive house on the estate is arguably 1 Boyne Park, which is by E.J. May, an architect of national repute who, in an interesting link, was the last pupil of the elderly Decimus Burton. May collaborated with Norman Shaw in the early "Garden Suburb" of Bedford Park in London. In Boyne Park, May designed in a Queen Anne style, and the way in which the building effortlessly fits the restricted site is masterly. The attractive original drawings show the complex roof plan and the various social requirements of the period, including a space for bicycle, a billiards room, butler's pantry and servant's room.

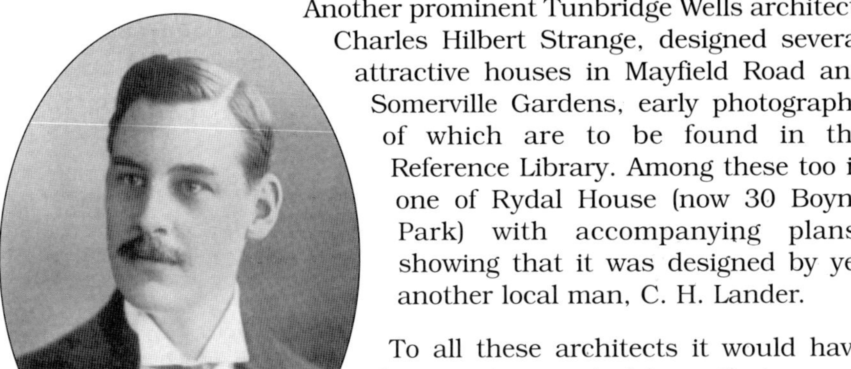

Charles Hilbert Strange.

Another prominent Tunbridge Wells architect, Charles Hilbert Strange, designed several attractive houses in Mayfield Road and Somerville Gardens, early photographs of which are to be found in the Reference Library. Among these too is one of Rydal House (now 30 Boyne Park) with accompanying plans, showing that it was designed by yet another local man, C. H. Lander.

To all these architects it would have been inconceivable that any householder on the estate would have done his own decorating, or his wife her own cooking and housework. In that direction there have been great changes, but on the whole the estate has been fortunate and has altered relatively little in outward appearance over the past century. Changes which were certainly not improvements were the removal of the attractive "barley sugar" design street lamps and their replacement by garish new lighting, and the substitution of pink tarmac for the brick pavements in parts of Oakdale Road and Mayfield Road. On the other hand, here as on the Molyneux Park estate there has been a reversal of the post-war trend to split these very large houses into flats. Three of those in Boyne Park and one in Oakdale Road have been converted back to single dwellings, one of them after having been divided into many units.

CHAPTER 6

WOODBURY PARK ROAD, PARK ROAD AND GROSVENOR PARK

by Susan Brown and Ann Bates

It appears that what was to be designated the Woodbury Park Development, was never intended to be other than a residential development, with no pretension of being a "park" in the Calverley or Nevill Park sense.

The area is titled "The Grosvenor Estate" on the 1838 Stidolph map, the Grosvenor family being early owners.

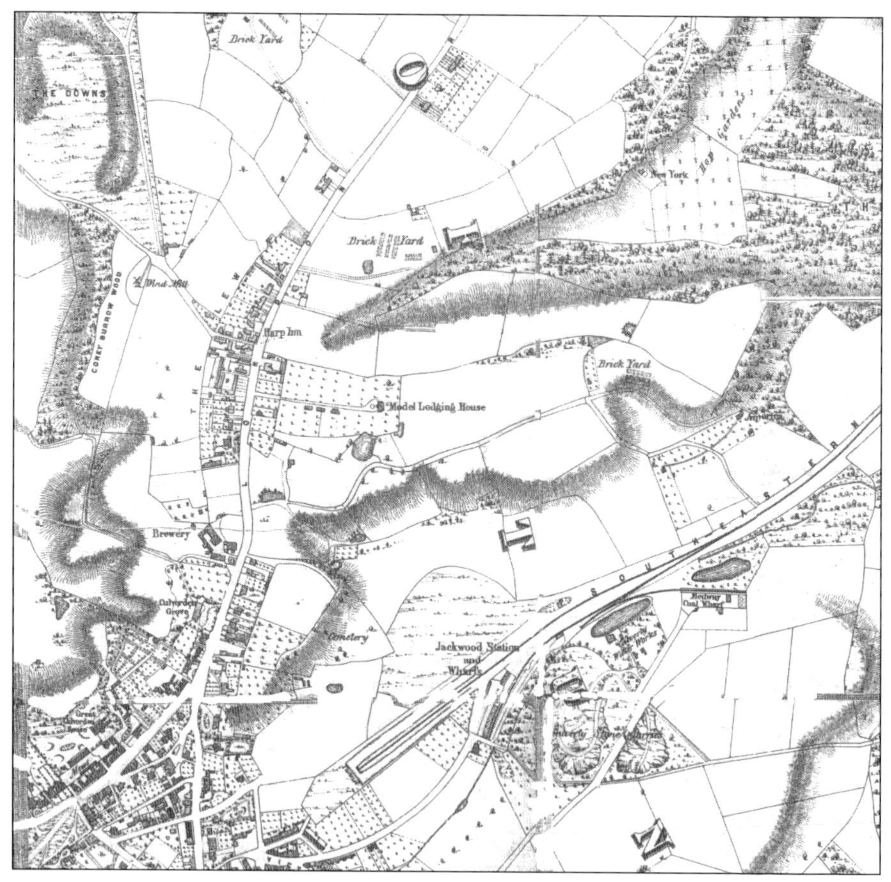

E. S. Gisborne: Plan of the TW Local Act District, 1849.

The first development of it was actually for a cemetery. The Woodbury Park Cemetery was opened in 1849 when the graveyard at Holy Trinity was full. The land had previously been fields belonging to John Waithman and among the subscribers who contributed to the purchase were John Deacon, John Ward and the Marquess of Abergavenny. The total expense, including the purchase of the land, enclosing and draining and erecting the little sandstone chapel came to around £1,200. The creation of the Cemetery and the carriage road leading to it from St. John's Road presumably gave the impetus for the development of the whole estate.

Built on sloping land and planted with evergreen trees and shrubs that give it a suitably sombre atmosphere, the cemetery filled rapidly and passed out of use by the end of the 19th. century, except for the occasional interment in family tombs. Among those buried here are Jacob Bell (Founder of the Pharmaceutical Society); William Willicombe (Builder and developer of much in Tunbridge Wells); Lt.General George Middlemore CB (Hero of the Battle of Talavera,1809); Sidney Smirke (1798-1877 (Architect with his brother of the British Museum and the Royal Academy); Canon Edward Hoare (Vicar of Holy Trinity); Rev. Henry Thomas Austen (Brother of Jane); Rev. William Law Pope (Minister of King Charles' Church); Charles Tattershall Dodd (Tunbridge Wells' only nationally-recognised artist); and a number of members of the Cripps family, but not W.C.Cripps, the first Town Clerk.

To quote Geoffrey Copus in one of the RTWCS Walks leaflets – "It is instructive to note that, in death as in life, our ancestors believed in keeping to their proper stations. The well-off huddle closely together on the heights and upper slopes, many commemorated by costly and elaborate monuments, and then there is a fringe of simple but substantial gravestones (many with excellent lettering) of tradesmen, lesser clergy and solid nonconformists. Finally, there is a large, somewhat chilling level area where lie those who, for the most part, have no memorial, who have vanished as if they had never been".(2) There are a total of 644 burials listed in the register for this little graveyard.

In 1856 the Conservative Land Society became owners of a large part of the Estate and chose to develop it for residential purposes under the name "The Woodbury Park Estate". The name means "a fortified place by a wood", but it is not yet known why this name was chosen.

The Conservative Land Society was a somewhat unusual 19th. century political organisation, whose aim was to try and control the outcome of local Parliamentary voting, by buying up land for upper middle /middle class development in specific constituencies, to ensure that only those who supported the Conservative party, were allowed to lease/buy properties within their ownership. It was made a condition of the lease/purchase that the buyer pledged his [not hers] political support for the Conservative party. The Society deliberately targeted areas for land-purchase where they deemed they wished to influence the political outcome in any Parliamentary election. Obviously, Tunbridge Wells came within this definition, particularly because the 1st. Marquess Abergavenny, who was the 'eminence grise' of the Conservative party at that time and had set up the National Union of Conservative Associations (which administratively has been responsible for ensuring that the Conservative party has ruled the country for 70 of the last 100 years), was a, if not the, local landowner.

The Conservative Land Society divided the sixty acres of land into lots which were offered as building plots, with Henry Pownall and Thomas Knox Holmes – Trustees for the Society – signing the conveyances. A letter which appeared in the Tunbridge Wells Gazette on 30th May 1856 mentions the plan and prospectus for the development as consisting of 75 lots, being sold for the total sum of £7,677. 6s. The writer surmises that as this comprised little more than half of the original estate as bought by the Company (i.e. Society), a tidy profit was being made. By December 1862 the Tunbridge Wells Journal was able to record that "all the gothic cottages...have been sold... and the four new roads are nearly finished". The cottages must refer to the "Model cottages" in Newcomen Road, designed by Henry Roberts, but the implication for the completion of the roads is that, at the least, building was about to begin.

The first edition Ordnance Survey map, printed 1867/8, shows "Woodbury Park" as covering plots on the south side of Queens Road down to Upper Grosvenor Road and the current Chilston Road is called Woodbury Crescent. On the east side of this stands "Greenbank", one of the earliest buildings in the area. William Afflick Jackson, a solicitor born in Lancashire in 1821, purchased the lots that the house and its pleasure grounds stood on. Some twenty years later, Jackson was embroiled in a court case because Winnifrith, a local builder, had bought adjoining plots and started building "Wingrove" and "Hamilton Lodge". Other owners and tenants had been consulted but not Jackson, who took legal action on the grounds that the new buildings affected the value of his property. The case ended up before the Vice-Chancellor at Lincoln's Inn. The verdict of "damages not proved" was given in June 1882.(1)

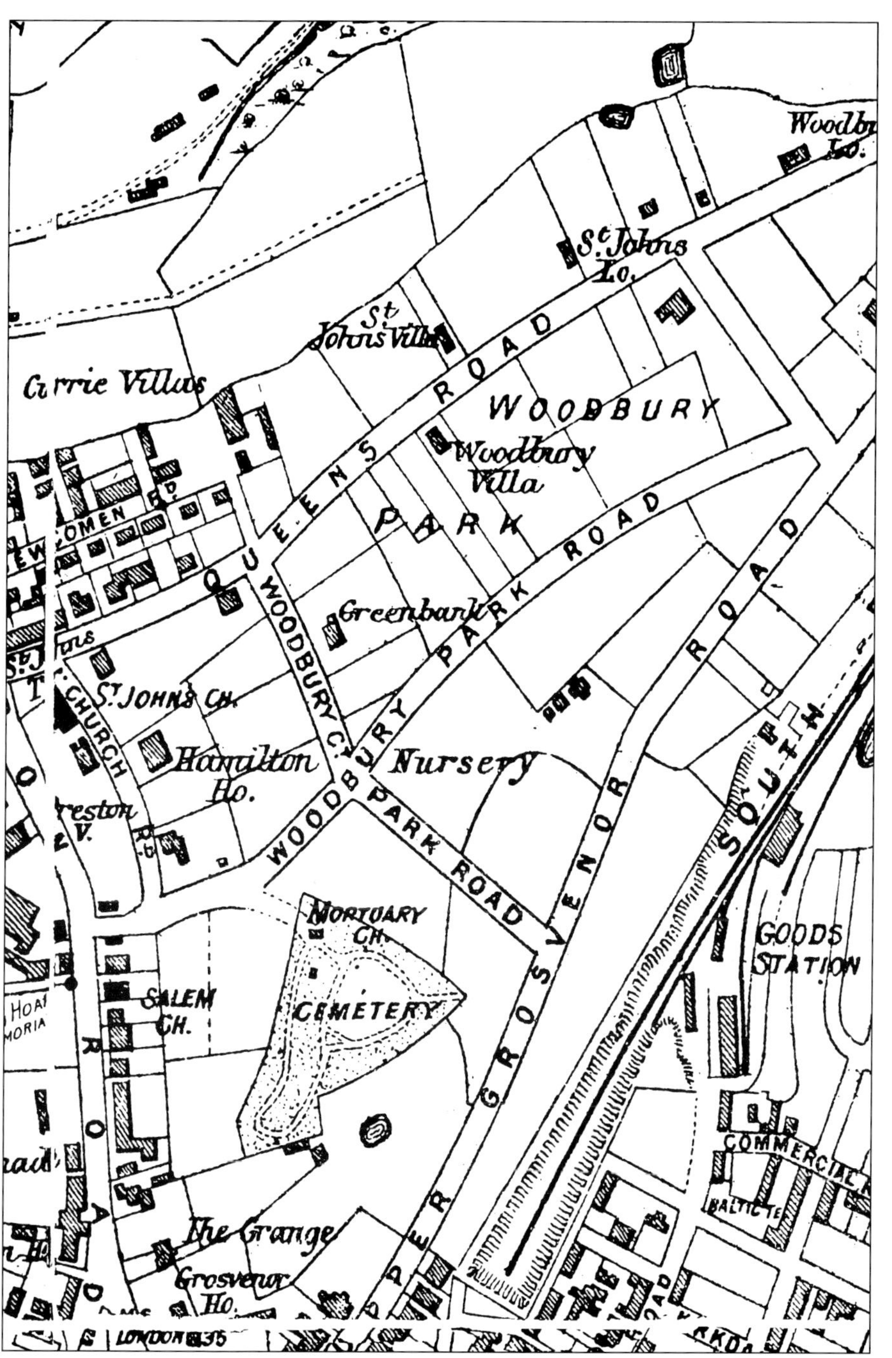

Woodbury Park in late 19th century.

Other than Greenbank, the 1867/8 Ordnance Survey map shows Woodbury Villa on Queens Road, and Woodbury Hill on the north-west corner of Dunstan Road (originally the boundary of the Woodbury Park Estate) and Woodbury Grange (roughly on the site of the present Woodbury Park Gardens). The latter was occupied for some years by a landscape gardener called William Rumbold. He sold the house in 1894. The house known as Wycliffe, (now No.7 Amherst Road and strictly speaking not part of the Woodbury Park development), was built between 1849 and 1866 in the "old English Manor style" of George Devey.

In 1863 the final allotment of 37 plots of the Woodbury Park development were offered for sale at £63 to £77, an advertisement in the Tunbridge Wells Gazette of 15th May 1863 stating that "several houses have been erected". Sales particulars for a kitchen garden on the corner of Dunstan Road in 1883 describe the plot as "one of the few remaining sites on the rapidly rising and favourite Woodbury Park Estate that can now be acquired". The second edition Ordnance Survey map, dated 1897, shows the whole development complete except for a few gaps around the north end of Park Road.

Woodbury Park Road, as such, is first listed on the 1871 Census. Amongst the residents were Alfred Hemstock at No.1 – a Commercial Traveller, Thomas Stidolph at No. 2 – a Coach Builder, Mary Corbett at No.3 – living off renting property, a couple of elderly ladies "supported by son" and the usual array of parlour maids and gardeners. At Newton House William Farmcombe from Solihull ran a school with the aid of his wife and niece, the children being of both sexes and ranging in age from 6 to 14.

In 1881 the Census listings reveal a typical picture of the town in the late Victorian period – well-to-do middle class families including retired tradesmen, colonial administrators and an Army tutor. Ten years later the Census for Walton Terrace, at the entrance to the Cemetery, shows a cricket ball maker (at No.3), and a "mechanical dentist" (at No.2). At "Penny-brin" (later to be 56 Woodbury Park Road) lived John Evans, Captain of the Bengal Staff, with his wife and six servants.

By the 1901 Census, the picture has changed a little – there are lodging houses, workers in various trades, those on independent means and, nearer St. John's Road, large houses with servants. No. 18 is Fry's mineral water factory and No. 37 is a Girls' school with eleven pupils.

The index of planning applications for the period reveals the names of some of the builders of Woodbury Park Road.

Charles Adie, who was responsible for a considerable amount of the residential development of the town in the 1870's and 1880's, applied for planning for Nos.26-40 in 1887/8 and for two houses on plot 5.

The name Edwards crops up several times and it is probably safe to assume that this applies to the firm of Edwards Bros., who moved into a new yard off Woodbury Park Road in c.1870. The yard appears to have been in the vicinity of Shirley Villas, near to the Cemetery. John Edwards moved into Clifton Cottage, which he had built for his own occupation (3) (4) and George Edwards into 1 Shirley Villas – which they had presumably erected themselves. Certainly they applied for planning permission for Nos.20-24 and other unidentified houses in 1877/8.

Another probable contender is Edmund Noakes, who had a builder's yard in Goods Station Road. He applied for No.60 in 1874 and was living in Woodbury Park Road, described as a retired builder, on the 1881 Census. This may well be the house later named as Omega House in 1891, when his widow was living there.

Woodbury Park Road exhibits a variety of architectural styles and was not developed in a uniform way. Walton Terrace, at the entrance to the Cemetery, is a pleasant red brick terrace with white pilasters decorating the windows and doors and with dormer windows decorated with bargeboards. Further down the road are pairs of large, yellow brick houses on the left and on the right several detached, red brick houses with a Gothic influence. After the remaining unsold plots were auctioned in 1895, the last houses in the development reveal the less forbidding influence of the Arts and Crafts movement.

Off Woodbury Park Road is Park Road, which began to be built up in the 1870's. Charles Adie put in for planning application for Nos.1-3 in 1876 and these houses match Nos.47-55 in Upper Grosvenor Road which were built at the same time – large villas with a high degree of ornamentation. Adie was declared bankrupt in 1877, having overreached himself with the development of the site of Grecian Villa off Claremont Road, and these plots were sold off either empty, or with uncompleted houses. It seems that Adie completed these houses and later built others, including Nos. 15/17 and 19/21, as his name appears under planning applications in 1887.

The name of Weare is listed as having applied for 2-12 Park Road, a name which appears elsewhere and may be John Smith Weare of Ferndale, who appears to have acquired much property in the town. There is also an application in the name of Wood in 1888, which must have been Charles Wood of 9 Park Road, who gives his occupation as "Builder" on the 1891 Census.

The 1891 Census for Park Road shows a high proportion of occupants living on independent means, about half of them widows. A retired army officer occupied the first of the large Adie houses, but the second shows only a caretaker and his family – the residents were presumably away. It is interesting to note that hardly any of the residents of the road at this date were actually born in Tunbridge Wells. A number give their place of birth as London or Surrey, which would seem to indicate that Tunbridge Wells had become a fashionable residential area.

From 1902-1938, "Agra House", 19 Park Road, was a Barnardo's Home. It is an interesting reflection on the changing nuances in the meaning of words, that Barnardo's was known in 1902 as the National Waifs' Association and No.19 as a 'Home for Little Incurables', both descriptions being entirely acceptable at the time, but subsequently changed to words with less emotionally-charged associations. It is also instructive that at that time, Barnardo's had 'already rescued, trained and placed out in life nearly 60,000 Orphan Waifs'; had 'emigrated to our Colonies 1,266 Boys and Girls during 1904'; and Barnardo's declared that '£16 will maintain a child in a Home for one year' and '£10 will cover all cost of emigrating one child'. Times have certainly changed.

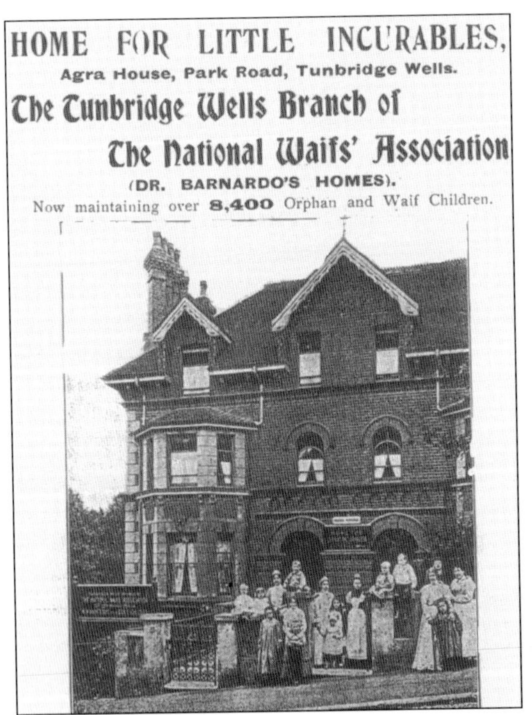

Agra House.

Charles Adie was also responsible for most of the development of Grosvenor Park. This road also stands on land that was originally part of the Grosvenor House Estate, the owner in 1835 being James Hockett Fry, a retired local butcher, who had inherited Grosvenor House from his father-in-law Joseph Delves.(5) In 1878, the Rev. James Fry (son of James Hockett Fry) sold the Estate to Adie, who submitted planning application for 14 houses in 1890 and for another 19 in 1891.

By the time the 2nd edition Ordnance Survey map was published in 1897, the road was fully built up except for a few gaps in the terraces which were developed at a later date. Sometime during this period Grosvenor House had been demolished.

Near the Grosvenor Road end of Grosvenor Park stands the Friends' Meeting House, which was built in 1894. The architects were C.E. Clayton & E. Black of Brighton. The number of members of the Society of Friends had been growing significantly since 1886 and a campaign to raise money for a much-needed building to house the group began in 1893. The final cost of the building was £2,100.

Opposite is a small chapel, listed in the street directories for the end of the 19th. century as Grosvenor Hall, which has recently been converted to residential use.

CHAPTER 7

THE CHANGING CONCEPT AND THE CHANGING TOWN

ST. JAMES' PARK AND FERNDALE PARK, SHERWOOD PARK, SANDOWN PARK AND SANDHURST PARK

by Ann Bates and John Cunningham

As the 19th. century progressed, the concept of a Residential Park changed from a group of houses sharing the same private miniature park, to a road with large detached houses on large plots within a sylvan setting, then to the same with paired villas on somewhat smaller plots. Certainly not all leafy roads in Tunbridge Wells were called Park. Indeed St. James' Road and neighbouring Lansdowne Road were to have substantially larger houses and plots than St. James's Park, which was developed 20-30 years later than either of them.

Tunbridge Wells expanded from a population of just over 8,000 in 1841 to nearly 30,000 in 1891, helped considerably by the arrival of the Railway in 1846. The expansion was mainly to the north and north-east behind Calverley Park or more precisely Calverley New Town, and between what is now St. John's Road and Pembury Road, but all within the extensive bounds of the Ward estate.

In the 1850's, Beulah Road (then called Hydraulic Road) was developed – with middle-class housing, while working-class cottages began to spring up in Quarry Road, Goods Station Road and elsewhere in the parish of Holy Trinity, then the only parish for the area. By the mid-1850s, the area had a considerable population of mixed classes which led, with the support of Canon Hoare, the Evangelical vicar of Holy Trinity Church, to the formation of new parishes in this area. St. John's was the first to be built in 1858, followed by St. James' in 1860-62 to a design by Ewan Christian FRIBA (1814-1895), and then on the fringe of the area, by St. Peter's in 1874-75. In their turn, the creation of the parishes encouraged more population and more housing.

Although there were already houses in the vicinity of St. James' Church, St. James' Road only started to develop after the Church was built. The 1867 Ordnance Survey map shows six detached houses and six semi-detached houses on the east side; and three detached houses and 14 semi-detached houses on the west. The development continued down the hill which is St. James' Road and as it crossed Albion Road,

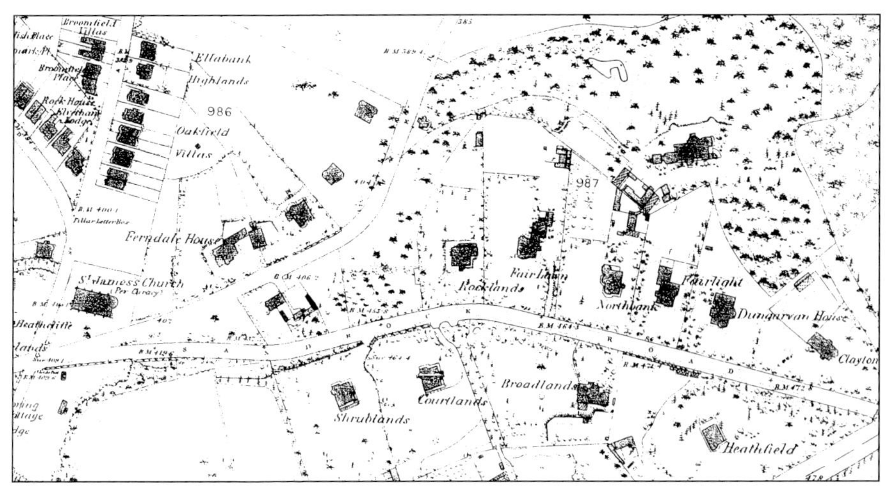

St. James' and Ferndale – Ordnance Survey Map, 1867.

the houses and gardens became smaller. By the 1897 edition, the OS map shows 21 detached and 42 semi-detached houses in St. James' Road down to Albion Road; and the road had been extended beyond Albion Road with about 8-10 shops, three detached, 28 semi-detached houses and a Public House – The Mitre, whose name has remained unchanged since it was built in 1872-3. Much of the development in the lower part of St James' Road was by Frederick James Castle, who had bought for £3,000 what was called the St. James' Estate, which included the land which is now the present day Auckland, Vernon and Rochdale Roads. Much of the building was carried out for him by George Mercer of nearby Goods Station Road.

(As a parochial aside, it should be recorded that the Inaugural meeting of the Royal Tunbridge Wells Civic Society, or The 59 Society as it was first known, was held at 4 St. James' Road on 17th. June 1959.)

St. James' Park, which runs off the eastern side of St. James' Road and has entrances from both St. James' Road and Albion Road, was a fairly late development of paired villas in the early 1890s. The 1897 OS map shows 26 houses built at the lower Albion Road end of the Park occupying less than a fifth of the site, but by 1909 the site was substantially complete. The villas are arranged in a curve on sloping ground and from certain viewpoints can be seen against a backdrop of trees. There is a general consistency of style among the red, or red and yellow villas, but they do differ in detail. For example, Nos. 31-45 have colonnettes to the bay windows and shaped arches to the window heads. Some of the villas, such as Hughenden Villas at Nos. 11-13, were given names and Nos. 59-61 bear the date 1899.

Ferndale (called over time variously Park and Road) was also influenced by the foundation of St. James' Church. Indeed St. James' Vicarage was originally at No.1 Ferndale, which was next door to the Church.

Ferndale started to develop in the early 1860s, but its development was not straightforward. The 1867 OS map shows that Ferndale was originally the track leading to Charity Farm a few hundred yards further north, which was part of the Dorking Charity Lands. Off this track on the right-hand side was The Dell, a large property with lake and woods, which was probably built in the 1850s. The Dell had its main entrance, which was guarded by a lodge, onto Ferndale; and a second entrance with a long drive onto Pembury Road. The Dell was initially lived in by John Muggeridge and his family and six servants and in the 1873 Return of Owners of Land for Kent, John Muggeridge is shown as owning 436 acres (far from all being The Dell), producing rents of £692 a year i.e. £1.60 an acre, which suggests that it was mainly agricultural land which commanded a rent of about £1 an acre at that time. Subsequently, The Dell was lived in by Frank Weare, the son of John Smith Weare, the founder of the High Brooms Brick & Tile Co. In due course, The Dell became No. 4 Ferndale.

Ferndale House.

But before that, and before he founded the High Brooms Brick & Tile Co. in 1885, John Smith Weare lived on the opposite side of the road at Ferndale House, No.3 Ferndale. The 1873 Return of Owners of Land shows him as owning 19 acres (probably in the vicinity of No.3) producing a rental of £294 a year, i.e. £15.47 an acre, which indicates that it was probably residential property.

On the other side of The Dell was Sandrock Road, which runs from St. James' Church to Pembury Road and has houses of a park-like nature. Sandrock Road was largely built by William Willicombe. The houses were smaller than The Dell but were nonetheless substantial and set in large gardens – Rocklands, Fairlawn, Northbank, Fairlight, Dungarvan House and Clayton House on the northern (Dell) side of the road; and Shrublands, Courtlands, Broadlands and Heathfield on the southern – all of them built about the same time in the 1860s. The northern side remains largely intact – with Rocklands now prominent as the Constitutional Club – and only Dungarvan House and Clayton House have been demolished to make way for the new road, Cleveland. But on the southern side, most have been demolished to make way for more intensive developments, including St.James' Primary School.

The track from St. James' Church which became Ferndale did not originally branch right as the main section of Ferndale now does towards Sandhurst Road, but carried on towards Charity Farm and this section is now called Hilbert Road. The main section of Ferndale only developed into a road as new houses were built by John Smith Weare in the 1870s and 1880s in what was by then called Ferndale Park, but there would not seem to have been any initial intention of driving it through to Sandhurst Road which was then little more than a track. However, sometime in the 1870s a large house called initially Sandhurst and subsequently Sandhurst Park, was built for John Smith Weare with its lodge on the western side of this track, which then became Sandhurst Lane and, by the 1890s, Sandhurst Road.

By 1886, there were 33 detached houses with large gardens on the western 'odd-number' side of Ferndale and on the 'even-number' side only seven which were even more substantial with much larger gardens. The breakthrough to Sandhurst Lane came in the early 1890s, prior to the proposed Liptraps Park Estate in 1893.

The number of houses in Ferndale remained unchanged until after the Second World War, when the size of the existing plots were to lead to substantial demolition and redevelopment. This included a new through road from Sandrock Road to Ferndale called Cleveland; and a large number of cul-de-sacs called Closes and Walks.

Kelsall Lodge, No. 29 Ferndale, which was designed by George Devey and built in 1869, and was a listed building, was the last to be demolished following a Public Inquiry in 1979. It was notable for its mullioned windows, its diaper-patterned brickwork and the interesting arrangement of chimney stacks.

Kelsall Lodge.

While the OS maps for both 1867 and 1897 record Ferndale as a Road, Bracketts

1936 Advertisement.

in their 1873 Compendium refer to the whole area as Ferndale Park 'one of the choicest localities in the town' overlooking ' a lovely valley bounded by a distant landscape of vast extent and singular beauty'. Confusion over the name arose in the 1930s when the Charity Farm land was developed as the Ferndale Park Estate, but which today is known as Hilbert Road, Ravenswood Avenue, Fairfield Avenue, Lipscombe and Pinewood Roads. These roads were built in 1935-6 and properties were offered at 'from £848' for detached houses and 'from £705' for semi-detached houses, 'including law costs'.

As the town expanded, developments spread outwards particularly along the Pembury Road, previously known as Calverley Fairmile, which with its very large houses and grounds had become 'The Millionaire's Row' of Tunbridge Wells.

Three of these developments are of relevance in the context of Residential Parks – in chronological order, Sherwood Park, Sandown Park and Sandhurst Park (and with the latter, the largely abortive Liptraps Park Estate).

Sherwood Park as an estate of some 60 acres, according to the Return of Owners of Land for 1873, lay on the northern side of Pembury Road between the present Sandhurst Road and Blackhurst Lane. The mansion was built in the 1860s at the northern end of the estate, closer to Blackhurst Lane. It was designed in the Italianate style also favoured in Hungershall Park. It was acquired in 1874 by Mr. (later Sir) William Siemens, FRS, and he lived there until his death in 1883, his widow continuing there until she died in 1901.

William (or more accurately Wilhelm) Siemens was born in 1823 in Hanover, the fourth of eight sons of a farmer. He was a metallurgist and electrical engineer and a very shrewd businessman, who in his lifetime was granted 113 British patents, ranging from electro-plating, steel manufacturing (by the Siemens process which rivalled the Bessemer system), transatlantic submarine cable, dynamos, transmission of power by electricity and refrigeration. He first came to England in 1843, was naturalised in 1859 and was knighted in 1883, only seven months before his death.

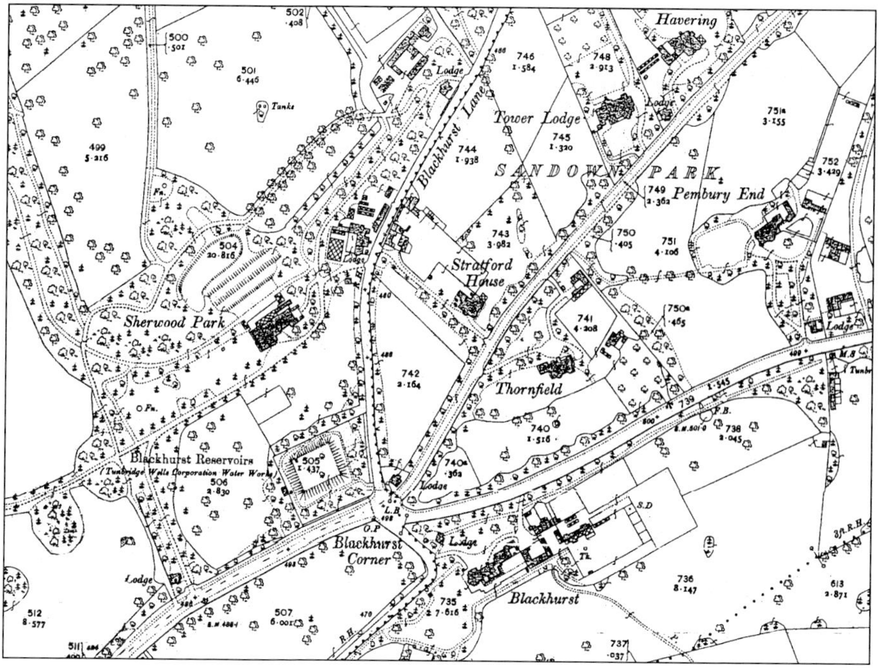

1897 Ordnance Survey map of Sandown Park, with Sherwood Park on middle left.

Sherwood Park became Sherwood Park Spa & Clinic in 1932, following the discovery of a new spring in its grounds whose water was claimed to be similar to that of Nauheim in Germany, which was noted for treatment of heart conditions. Lady Ottoline Morrell, the famous 'Bloomsberry' (who was the friend and mentor of Bertrand Russell, Aldous Huxley, Axel Munthe, Augustus John, Duncan Grant and Lytton Strachey), died at the Clinic in April 1938, following the suicide of her doctor, Dr. Cameron. The Clinic survived only until the Second World War, when Sherwood Park became a maternity and nurses' home for Kent County Council before being taken over by the Tunbridge Wells District Health Authority.

Sherwood Park, later Cumberland Park.

In the early 1950s, part of the Park adjoining Sandhurst Road was sold to Tunbridge Wells Borough Council for Council housing. Over 400 houses were built and the estate was called Sherwood.

The Sherwood Park mansion reverted to residential use in

2000 when it was converted into flats and its name was changed to Cumberland Park, probably to avoid confusion with the Sherwood Estate.

Close to Cumberland Park is Sandown Park which was a private gated road with an entrance lodge; and which consisted of half-a-dozen substantial houses in large grounds, some with their own lodge as well. Pelton's Guide of 1874 says 'Sandown Park lies a mile and a half from the town, between Pembury Road and Blackhurst Lane, and will probably, from its elevated position and magnificent views, become a favourite building ground'. This forecast did not quite prove itself to be true, at least in the 19th. century. The first house in the Park would seem to be Pembury Grange which was built in 1869 and the other five appear to have followed somewhat later in the late 1870s and 1880s.

Pembury Grange

Originally called Calverley Grange after its first owner's family associations, Pembury Grange was designed for Neville Ward, one of the two sons of John Ward for whom Decimus Burton had laid out Calverley Park a generation earlier. Its architect, George Devey (1820-1886) was one of the most important and successful country-house architects in England at that time. Devey had been the inspired choice of architect by Philip Sidney, 2nd. Lord De L'Isle and Dudley, for extensive works to the Buckingham Building and other parts of nearby Penshurst Place.

As Dr. Philip Whitbourn has written: 'At Pembury Grange, Devey designed in the vernacular Kentish tradition, with different combinations of brick, stone, tile-hanging, rough-cast and half-timbering beneath a series of gables of differing heights. The resulting effect, while forming a coherent unified composition, shows also the Devey trademark of giving the appearance of an ancient house which has grown organically through additions made over the years.'

The question arises as to whether Neville Ward was hoping in Sandown Park to repeat some of his father's success with Calverley, but there does not appear to have been a comprehensive plan to do so. The other houses followed slowly and at five in number, were certainly less than the site could have accommodated.

Sandown Park.

The house which originally took the name Sandown Park was designed by Reginald Pope of Folkestone and seems to have changed its name to Tower Lodge fairly early on, possibly to avoid confusion with the name for the area.

Stratford House in Sandown Park was occupied by Julius Caeser, a merchant and naturalised British citizen of German birth. Stratford House later changed its name to Sandown Court and subsequently was demolished and a school with the same name was built on the site. Havering House also changed its name to Summerlands and is now demolished, but Thornfield House survives, surrounded by new developments.

Pembury Grange, which is Grade II listed, also survives but is now divided into several houses, called Devey House, Devey Court and Devey Gables. The last house in the Park, Pembury End, which always had an entrance from the Pembury Road, is now part of the Cheshire Homes Seven Springs complex.

The Sandown Park area has been substantially developed since the Second World War. The gated entrance has gone, but the estate still retains a leafy aspect.

Sandhurst Park was the last, by only a short margin, to be developed and it certainly did not achieve the promise it could have had under the name of Liptraps Park.

The Sandhurst Park area was adjacent to High Brooms which since the 1840s had become a centre for brick-making due to the large deposits of Wadhurst clay, which was ideal for brick-making, in the vicinity. A number of brickworks had existed, but it was the establishment in 1885 of the High Brooms Brick & Tile Co. Ltd. close to the railway line, which was probably a major factor in the decision by the railway company to create a new railway station on the Tonbridge – Tunbridge Wells line.

Plan of proposed estate, 1893.

Besides providing a siding for loading bricks, the station was intended to serve the inhabitants of Southborough, which was a mile distant, and the growing number of residents in the north of the town of Tunbridge Wells. The new railway station was called Southborough and opened in 1893 and remains so to this day, but under the name of High Brooms to which it was changed in 1925.

It is speculation, but the sudden death of John Smith Weare in 1890 at the relatively early age of 62, may have had some influence on these developments.

Sandhurst (Park), the house in which he lived at his death, was less than half-a-mile from the new railway station as the crow flies; and the land in-between of about 150 acres was wood and fields. So it is not surprising that this acreage could be seen as an opportunity for a major piece of development when a new railway station was being so conveniently proposed. It was planned to call the development Liptraps Park after the farm on the site and if it had ever been properly achieved, it would have been the largest development to date in Tunbridge Wells – about 50% larger than Warwick Park in terms of acreage, but two to three times larger in terms of the number of houses, because of the proposed mix of housing.

The Estate would have had 11 roads to service a total of 230 plots. At the top of the Estate, closest to Sandown Park, would have been 19 plots varying in size from 1½ to 7 acres, intended to be developments of a style suited to the Pembury Road area. Further down the hill were a another 211 plots of increasingly diminishing size as one approached the station. Some 108 of the 230 plots were clearly intended, by the size of the plots and their proximity to the railway line, to be less affluent housing.

It was an enormously ambitious plan and one that could have succeeded if it had been on a somewhat smaller scale and if the finance for it had not literally died. Some of it was completed – about six of 19 large plots and about 80 of the 108, which are now Clifton Road and Oak Road – but much of the site was not to be developed until after the Second World War.

Who was behind this ambitious development? The architect was William Barnsley Hughes (1852-1927) and the finance for the development was provided by Francis Peek, a member of the Peek, Frean biscuit-making family and a property developer, who financed a number of Hughes's projects. Hughes was born in 1852 near

Birmingham, the son of a bricklayer who had risen to the position of gas works manager. By the age of 21, he was in partnership in Tunbridge Wells as an architect and surveyor with James Weeks, the son of George Weeks, the builder. At the age of 23, he married his partner's sister, Ellen, and by the age of 26, he and his partner were working with Francis Peek. The association with Peek provided commissions outside Tunbridge Wells, but also meant that finance was available for projects inside the town.

Among his works in Tunbridge Wells are Brunswick Terrace; nos. 31-63a Mount Sion; the Methodist Chapel (now demolished) and the Friendly Societies' Hall, both in Camden Road; the Royal Kentish Hotel (now Kentish Mansions) in London Road; and the magnificent stable block for Sir David Salomons at Broomhill. He also obtained the commission to design the new railway station for Southborough/High Brooms, which no doubt gave him the insight and the inspiration to produce the plan for the Liptraps Park Estate.

Francis Peek died in 1899, which led to the finance for Liptraps drying up. So an imaginative plan never achieved its potential.

The present Sandhurst Park is a crescent-shaped road, off Sandhurst Road, where one of the early Liptraps houses, Sundal, survives.

The adjoining land of Sherwood Park was to be developed for Council housing in the 1950s, and a large part of what could have been Sandhurst or Liptraps Park, was absorbed after the Second World War and following the closure of the High Brooms Brick & Tile Co. in 1968, into what became the North Farm Industrial estate.

CHAPTER 8

LINDEN PARK, MADEIRA PARK AND WARWICK PARK

by Ann Bates and John Cunningham

The area where these three 'parks' were to be developed in the late 19th and early 20th centuries was land originally in the parish of Frant and mainly owned by the Abergavenny Estate of Eridge.

All three started development over a period of ten years 1886-1896 and the principal reason for them was that there was an agricultural recession in Britain in the 1880-90s, due mainly to cheap meat and wheat coming in from North and South America. The Marquess of Abergavenny was capital-rich with 30,000 acres, but in the 1880s and 1890s suffered a dramatic fall in income from £50,000 to £40,000 a year as a result of the recession. The three developments were specifically designed to restore his income, since he knew that his urban land in Tunbridge Wells could generate average rents of £12 an acre, where his agricultural lands only averaged £1 an acre.

The three Parks varied considerably in size. Linden Park and Madeira Park were relatively small and were the first to start development. Warwick Park, initially at 134 acres although subsequently reduced to 99 acres, was potentially the largest development in the history of the town.

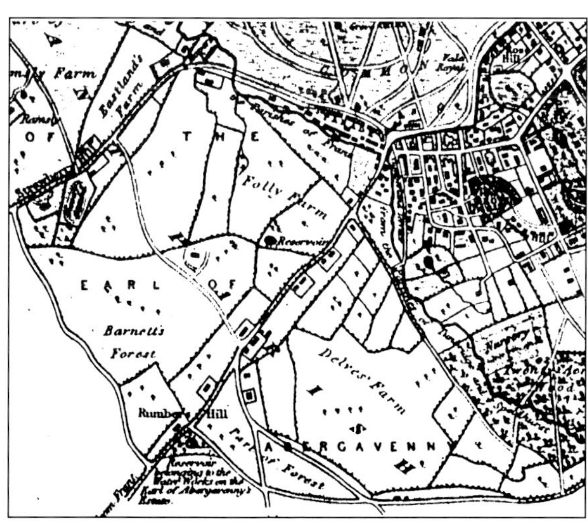

Detail of Stidolph's 1838 map, showing Folly Farm, Delves Farm and the Madeira Park site.

In the 19th and early 20th. centuries unlike today, most houses were built for renting. As a result, they were usually built speculatively and in small numbers as the return from renting took up to 20 years to return the investment. So it was quite usual for a road to be developed slowly, 2-5 houses at a time, so as not to overstretch the 'cash-flow'.

Stidolph's map of 1838 shows the land where Linden Park was to be developed from 1886, as fields and a farm nearby named Folly Farm. On the later Ordnance Survey map of 1868/73 there is a track with the Royal Victoria Brewery on ground to the west and to the south is New Station Road, which was to become Montacute Road. On the 1897 O/S map Linden Park is established, with Madeira Park sketched in, and where Warwick Park was to be built, there are fields belonging to what is variously called Home Farm/Delves Farm. It is not until the map of 1909 that all three roads are shown as being developed.

In Pelton's Illustrated Guide to Tunbridge Wells, there is the following description 'unbeneficial clergymen, gentlemen who have served their country in the army, in the navy, or in colonial appointments, and retired merchants, have settled in large numbers in this quiet, healthy and lovely spot. It is also a favourite residence for widows and maiden ladies of independent means.'

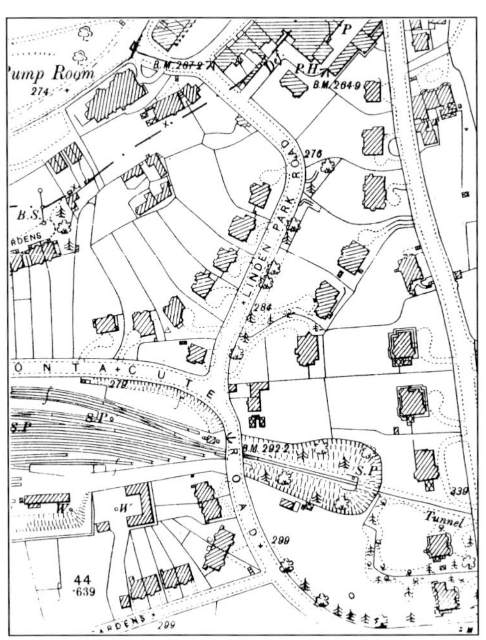

1897 OS map showing Linden Park site.

The first planning applications for Linden Park were made to the Tunbridge Wells Works Committee in 1886 when Beale and Sons submitted plans for a new road and alterations to drainage and for four houses. In the following years, a further ten houses were built in two phrases. The houses are built on rising ground and behind them is Frant Road.

The description of Madeira Park by Alan Savidge in his book 'Royal Tunbridge Wells', could also be applied to Linden Park: 'in this estate, [Councillor] Beale and Sons built large red brick houses, sprouting gables, turrets, balconies, black and white timbering, tile-hanging, in Edwardian profusion'. It is unclear who the architect for Beale was at this time, but in the planning applications Beale seems to have been architect, developer and builder.

In the 1901 census there is some confusion as to which road some of the houses were situated in, Linden Park (now in the parish of King Charles the Martyr), or Frant Road. This is also reflected in the planning applications made to the Borough Council.

Louis Beale moved in 1912 from 6, Madeira Park which had been the estate office for the firm, to Linden, Linden Park where he lived until about 1933.

The residents of the houses as mentioned by Pelton's included professional and wealthy businessmen. In the 1891 and 1901 censuses, there are many references to persons living on own means, one of whom was Henry Edmunds aged 38 born in the U.S.A. Living at No. 8 was Edward Durrent aged 66 years, born at Becking Essex. Durrent's was a well known grocery shop on The Pantiles, until it ceased trading in the 1950s.

The road was within easy reach of both the West Station [Brighton line] and the Central Station [London – Hastings line] and was ideal for the City businessman, who by this time was beginning to move out into the country, hopefully to live in park-like surroundings. But in reality their houses were just in rather grand suburban roads. None of the three roads which we are discussing had 'land not to be built upon' in their layouts, which had given an open park-like area to the earlier developments in the Town, although all had covenants restricting the residents' behaviour and future development.

Throughout the early part of the 20th century the road changed very little. More houses were built by other builders, one of which was No. 12, built by Strange and Sons, a well known builder/developer in Tunbridge Wells. In 1936 a new Christian Science Church was built on the west side of the road at the end nearest The Pantiles. In 1956 the St. Johns Road branch of the Christian Science Church joined the Pantiles branch, releasing their building in St. John's Road, designed by Cecil Burns, to become offices for the Freight Transport Association. In the late 1980s the Corn Exchange in the Lower Pantiles was redeveloped by Speyhawk and a new Auction Room was built in the development for Bracketts, who had previously held weekly auctions in the Corn Exchange. This is now [2004] Dreweatt and Neate's Auction Hall.

The whole area of Madeira Park is on a steep hill descending from Claremont Road to Warwick Park. The road divides at the top only to join up again before becoming Rodmell Road. On the north side of the road there are retaining walls of the local sandstone. The road has remained a quiet residential road, with many trees, giving a woodland-like setting, but the central island of land which theoretically could have been a Park, was built on from almost the very beginning.

In April 1893, Beale and Sons made the first application for the development of Madeira Park for new roads and sewers but it was not until November 1893 that plans for the four houses were passed. Some 33 houses were to be built in the following eight years. In all, there were 74 plots planned by Beale, but not all were developed, and Beale was to be responsible for 35 houses of the 39 built before the First World War. When No. 46 was advertised to be auctioned in 1898 it was described as 'so desirably situate on an eminence, in a central and cheerful position, within a few minutes of the Southern and the London, Brighton and South Coast Stations'. It did not sell and was withdrawn at £2050. Only 60 detached houses were finally built over some forty years, the last house to be built by Beale and Sons being No. 58 in 1926/27.

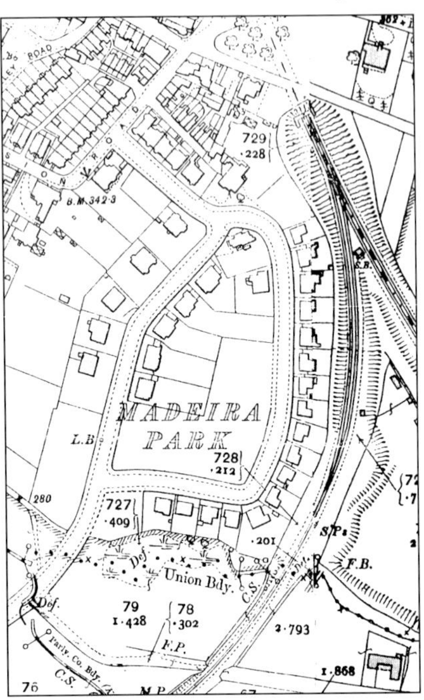

1909 OS map of Madeira Park

Beale would seem to have been a very good salesman – his advertising for Madeira Park claimed somewhat optimistically that it was 'about three minutes from the Pantiles and the South Eastern Railway Station.' Obviously, the Victorians walked much faster than we do today.

Other builders/developers included W. Leonard, E. R. Walker, and F. Featherstone. In more recent times there has been further building especially at the Rodmell Road/Warwick Park junction, and some of the larger properties have been converted into flats.

The 1901 census record residents who were well known in Tunbridge Wells. These included at No. 5, Richard Pelton who was the publisher of the Pelton Guides and Directories, living with his wife and family, a cook and housemaid; at No. 6, Mary A. Beale and Louis Beale, the developer and builder. with a son described as builders assistant. (In the directories, No. 6 is described as the estate office of Beale and Sons, with their builder's yard in Birling Road.). At No.18, there was an actress [!] Gertrude Kennedy with two sons and two daughters; at No. 19, Reuben Hall, bookseller, who was the founder of Hall's Bookshop which is still in business in Chapel Place; and at No. 45, Henry Wickenden, auctioneer. In February 1903, plans were submitted by Rev. A. W. Oliver for a vicarage for Kings Charles the Martyr in Madeira Park, but it was subsequently built in Frant Road.

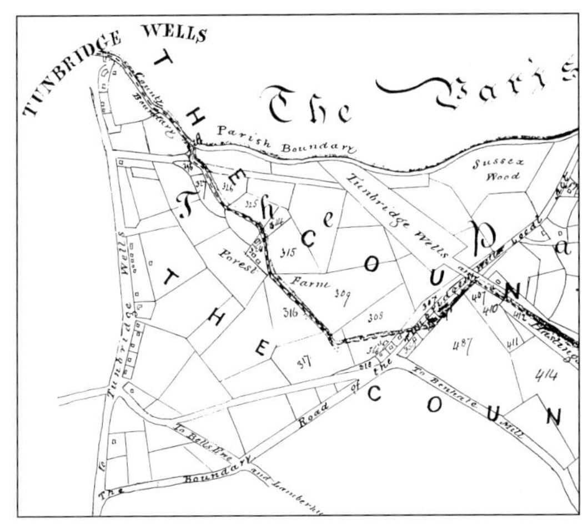

Frant Tithe map of c.1855.

While Linden Park and Madeira Park continued to be developed, the Marquess of Abergavenny was making plans to develop his land known at the time as Home Farm, but previously as Delves Farm and Forest Farm, which was still largely but not entirely in the county of Sussex. This consisted of all the land between Nevill Street in the west, Forest Road in the east, Frant Road in the south, and to the north beyond the London – Hastings railway line. Like Linden Park and Madeira Park, the Home Farm estate is on a very hilly site.

Home Farm had been leased for many years to the Delves Family, well known in the development and life of Tunbridge Wells from the mid-18th. century. The Delves family started as butchers in the Pantiles and Chapel Place, but over time expanded their interests to include property and other well-known Tunbridge Wells businesses, such as banking.

They seem to have held the lease of Home Farm from about 1800 and it is reasonable to assume with their butcher's business, that the farm was used in the days before refrigeration as a 'fattening pen' for stock awaiting slaughter. It probably helped that the then-current 'paterfamilias', William Delves, had become Steward to the Marquess in 1844.

But the Delves seem to have given up the lease of Home Farm about 1870, probably because the need for a 'fattening pen' had diminished.

Smithfield Market in London had changed in 1866 from being a 'live-animal' market to being a 'dead-meat' market; and with the coming of the telegraph and the railways, meat could be delivered within 4-5 hours of its order, so the need for a 'fattening pen' had declined considerably. The coming of refrigeration, together with refrigerated supplies arriving from North and South America, reduced the need even further.

With the Delves' no longer holding the head-lease, the Home Farm fragmented into a number of relatively short-term leases and it is therefore not surprising that when the Marquess had his 'cash-flow' problems in the 1880-90s, the site which was less than 100 yards from the Pantiles should become a prime opportunity for development.

The idea had been mooted for some time. A plan exists, based on an 1879 map of the Farm estate, which indicates how in theory the 134 acre site could be divided into 100 plots, but this took no account of the topography. So William Brackett was engaged to produce a thorough survey which he did in 1893. He estimated the total site as 135 acres, 3 roods and 6 perches.

A London architect, Henry Currey, was engaged and was to produce no less than three proposals. The first in which he proposed no less than 248 plots, clearly demonstrated that he had not understood the brief, which was to produce superior dwellings on significant acreage in the 'Eastbourne or Bournemouth' mould. His subsequent proposals were for 84 and 57 plots. But neither seem to have inspired confidence, and he vanished from the scene. He was replaced by William Roper, a local surveyor who knew and understood the site, and whose proposals went forward.

Mr. William Roper.

In February 1896 the Marquess advertised in the Courier under the heading 'Eridge Estate New Road' which invited tenders 'in connection with the making of New Roads, Sewers, Storm Water Drains, Brick Pavements etc.' to be submitted by Saturday 29th February 1896. The contract was awarded on 23rd November 1896 to Walter Arnold and Sons of Frant. The amount agreed to was £13,292 – 5s – 3d, but Arnold's original tender was £15,049-1s-

11d, so the Marquess (or more specifically, his Agent, George Macbean) drove a hard bargain. In the original specification as many as six roads were specified, although in the end only four were constructed.

The 'Plots for Sale' prospectus produced by William Roper appeared in January 1897, at a notional 65 plots, which, apart from the relatively tentative Liptraps Park proposal (see Chapter 7) was by far the largest estate planned in Tunbridge Wells up to this time. However, the Marquess did not intend to be the builder/developer but rather to provide the infrastructure for roads and sewers to service the plots.

The southern part of the estate was developed first, with only a few initially on the northern side. The main development of the northern part above Roedean Road was to take place after the First World War and even after the Second World War.

The development of Warwick Park was taken territorially by a number of developer/builders. Beale was to take the road below Rodmell Road, building nos. 6-36 before the First World War. Blatchington Road was essentially the work of Henry Vaux Wild, as developer and Thomas Bates as his builder. Roedean Road and the corner into Warwick Park had a number of developers, with Thomas Bates as their builder. But there was no single dominant builder for the Estate.

By 1914, 78 houses had been built on the 65 plots. Many of the houses were semi detached. Amongst the builders/developers, Beale and Sons built 15 houses between 1898 – 1904. Strange and Sons were to build Nos. 38, 40, 64-70 and 76 and 78. Thomas Bates built Nos. 80-88 and also Cliffe House (No.67) and Cliffe Cottage in the years 1898-1901. Among the developers were Henry Vaux Wild [15], S.E.Haward [6], C.Crisford [5] W.S.Putland [4] H.Dear [3] and E. Drewitt [2].

Beale subsequently built Nos. 94-112 (but not No. 100) after the the First World War, together with Nevill Gate, which he shared with Thomas Bates. Thomas Bates was also to build 'Brookside' in 1922 and Nos.57-59. Many other houses were built by individuals and developers, at various dates through out the 20th century.

Throughout the period up to 1909 when the O/S map shows Warwick Park as Warwick Road, there was much confusion as to what the new road should be called. In 1897 King Charles Road is referred to, a little later it is Home Park Road and it was not until 1900 that it was renamed Warwick Park, probably after the family connection of the Abergavenny's with the Earls of Warwick (both bear the surname Nevill). Other roads on the Home Farm estate (Roedean, Blatchington and Rodmell) were named after other estates in Sussex owned by the Marquess.

Some notable buildings in Warwick Park, include No.3, a red brick office/warehouse building with baroque decoration by the architect William Barnsley Hughes, which was built for wine merchants in 1900 but more recently has been the regional headquarters of the English Tourist Board. The builders were J. Laney and Son. Next door is Kings Charles' Parish Hall which is a modest but stylish red brick building by the architect Stanley Philpot, RIBA. Its foundation stone was laid by the 1st. Marquess in 1914 and it was completed in 1920.

Another notable house, Courtleas, No. 69, designed by the architect, W. Harold Hillyer and built by John Jarvis, is the only Neo-Georgian house in Warwick Park and is a close but smaller copy of Edwin Lutyens' Middlefield in Great Shelford, Cambridgeshire. Before designing Courtleas, which is believed to be his first independent commission, Hillyer worked with Sir Astin Webb, the leading Edwardian architect, on the design of the façade of Buckingham Palace in 1911, the Admiralty Arch in 1908, and the Victoria & Albert Museum in 1906. He was killed in 1916 during the First World War, having been the Royal Engineer officer in charge of the mining of Hill 60 at Ypres in April 1915, for which he received the MC.

Another aspect of interest concerning Courtleas is that it was requisitioned during the Second World War as the residence of the General Officer Commanding (GOC) of 12 Corps, which was headquartered in Tunbridge Wells and responsible for the defence of Kent and Sussex against any German invasion. Consequently, Lt.General Bernard Montgomery (subsequently to be Field Marshal Lord Montgomery of Alamein) lived there for eight months in 1941.

Cricket Week at the Nevill Ground c.1910.

The residents of Warwick Park listed in Pelton's Directory of 1902, included M. Saltmarsh; Percy Lankester, photographer; and E Drewett, developer. Amongst the others are widows, maiden ladies and retired gentlemen, a very similar range of residents to Madeira Park and Linden Park.

Besides the development of houses, in 1895 negotiations were started for land on the Home Farm estate to be developed as a cricket ground. County cricket had been played on the Common until 1884 when the incursion of roaming sheep proved too much. Tradesmen in the town regretted the loss of business and a new site was sought. But it took twelve years to find an acceptable one.

The Marquess offered twelve acres on the Warwick Park Estate at £7 an acre a year and as a result, the Tunbridge Wells Cricket, Football and Athletic Club Ltd. was set up with a capital of £10,000, not all of which was to be fully subscribed, to create the Nevill Ground. An additional problem was that the cost of developing the site, initially estimated at £5,000, proved eventually to be £13,493-12s-10d, largely due to having to turn a 12 acre slope into three flat pitches. The ground was opened before an estimated crowd of 12,000 on Whitsun Bank Holiday Monday, 30 May 1898, attended by the Marquess, and the elite of Tunbridge Wells. It was a popular success but a financial disaster for the 50 years for which the company survived, until they were bought out by the Borough Council. The problem was that that they were under-capitalised and under-subscribed from the very beginning and they never recovered.

But the Ground has always been popular. County cricket returned to Tunbridge Wells at the Nevill Ground in 1901 and has remained ever since with an annual Cricket Week at the end of May /beginning of June.

The burnt-out Cricket Pavilion, 1913.

Perhaps its most dramatic event was when the cricket pavilion, built by Strange & Sons, was burnt down on 13th. April, 1913. The Suffragette movement was blamed on circumstantial evidence and for weeks, the town was in uproar. For once, the Courier makes very interesting reading.

CHAPTER 9

GREAT CULVERDEN PARK

by John Cunningham

It may seem somewhat anomalous to include Great Culverden Park in this monograph about Residential Parks because its origin, its period of development and the intentions of those behind its development, were quite different from all the other Residential Parks featured in this monograph.

Great Culverden Park exists today as a private park of $9\frac{1}{2}$ acres of landscaped 'woodland', into which there is access from the back gardens of its neighbouring roads: Royal Chase, Culverden Park, Connaught Way and Knightbridge Close. It contains three ponds, called functionally Upper, Middle (or Tank) and Lower, the latter with a small island called Goose Island. It has a stream and an area designated as a playing field, but it has no tennis courts or cricket pitch, although both have been proposed but never implemented.

What makes it different from all the other Residential Parks in Tunbridge Wells is that the Park itself at $9\frac{1}{2}$ acres is much larger than most of the other Parks, with the possible exception of the original ones of Calverley, Nevill, Hungershall and Camden; and yet it was only created as such in 1936, which is about 100 years later than the original ones, by which time the concept of Park had generally evolved into a pleasant name for a nice quiet residential road.

It was also different from those Parks which were miniature parks insofar as its houses backed onto the Park, rather than fronting it. However this concept was not new. Indeed many of the developments of the Conservative Land Society (see Chapter 6) in the 19th. century, such as in St. Margaret's, Twickenham, backed onto a communal park or 'grounds', rather than fronting it.

But probably the biggest difference was that the residential roads were partly developed before the Park was created, which as far as the original principles of Residential Parks are concerned, is ' cart before horse'.

Nonetheless, Great Culverden deserves inclusion in this monograph, partly because it was in *effect* a very late (20th. century) 'throw-back' to the original thinking behind Residential Parks; partly because it is different, but nonetheless an integral part of Tunbridge Wells; and partly because although it did not start out to be a Residential Park, it has ended up being one.

How did it all happen?

The park takes its name from the house, called Great Culverden, which once stood on the ridge above it and whose site is now occupied by the Kent & Sussex Hospital. In medieval times, pigeons were known locally as 'culvers' and forest clearings were known as 'dens', so it is not surprising that when the first big house to be built on the ridge, was known as The Culverden House.

The Culverden House was built sometime between 1740 and 1760. The lease of this house and some adjoining land was acquired by Selina, the Dowager Countess of Huntingdon(1707-1791). In 1769 she built a chapel on the adjoining land for the sect of Methodists, whom she established and who took her name as Lady Huntingdon's Connexion. The Chapel flourished under the guidance of the Rev. George Whitefield (1714-1770) and subsequent ministers, and was enlarged several times, finally being transformed in 1867 into a stone building, called Emmanuel Church, with a 130 ft. spire which became one of the landmarks of Tunbridge Wells, until it was demolished in 1974 to give better road access to the Kent & Sussex Hospital.

Great Culverden in the 19th century.

Jacob Jeddere Fisher, called 'an engineer' which was unusual description in the early 19th. century, came from Ealing in Middlesex. He moved with his family of two sons and twin daughters to Tunbridge Wells in 1828 with sufficient money to buy The Culverden House, have it pulled down and engage Decimus Burton to design a new imposing residence, which he called Great Culverden. It is significant that Burton was designing this single house at exactly the same time as he was creating the 24 houses of Calverley Park.

Great Culverden

Great Culverden was similar but probably larger than those houses in Calverley Park. It was a square stone-built house rendered in cement and its size gives some indication of the position in Tunbridge Wells society to which the Fishers aspired.

Gardens and lawns sloped down from Great Culverden to a sandstone cliff, below which lay what is now the Park, then a small meadow valley with a stream. Jacob had the swampy areas excavated, drained and dammed to form the upper and lower ponds. He made other improvements, making a grotto, fencing with iron railings, building a little Swiss Cottage, and a tower, which was subsequently known as Fisher's Tower, or Culverden Castle. He also created an elaborate and ingenious Hydraulic Ram system to pump water hydraulically to the house with the middle pond acting as a header tank for the ram; and this system still exists, although no longer in use.

Sadly, Jacob did not live long enough to enjoy the fruits of his efforts. He died seven years after the completion of Great Culverden, but his widow, Elizabeth, lived there until her death in the 1870's.

The Great Culverden estate was then acquired by the Hon. James Byng, son of Vice-Admiral the 6th. Viscount Torrington. The Byng family, which had included in previous generations Admiral John Byng, court-martialled and executed in 1757 according to Voltaire 'pour encourager les autres', were a family with long-standing Tunbridge Wells associations.

James Byng died in May 1897 leaving the Great Culverden Estate to his grand-niece, Frances Russell Hall, who was married to Rear-Admiral Charles Lucas VC. Charles Lucas has the distinction of being the first holder of the Victoria Cross. Technically he is listed as fourth, since at the investiture by Queen Victoria in 1856, there were three winners senior to him in rank, but he was the first to earn the distinction when on 21st. June 1854 as a Midshipman on the paddle-wheel warship HMS Hecla, in an attack on Bomersund in the Baltic, as a northerly part of the Crimea War against Russia, he picked up an unexploded shell which had landed on the ship and threw it overboard, seconds before it exploded, and thus saved the ship. He was immediately promoted by his Admiral to Lieutenant and subsequently was the first person to be awarded the Victoria Cross.

Charles Lucas died three days after the start of the First World War on 7th August 1914 at the age of 80. His widow, Frances, continued to live at Great Culverden until her death in January 1925.

The Trustees of the Estate then tried to wind up the estate, putting it on the market as a whole, through Bracketts. The Estate was some 74 acres in total. At the auction, the bidding was disappointing and only reached £36,000, which was £4,000 below the reserve set by the Trustees. So the Estate was withdrawn.

For some time the Great Culverden Estate had slowly been surrounded by residential roads on both its northern and southern sides. To the north from 1880, the Culverden Park estate was developed as 'Gentlemen's Houses' on the West side of St. John's Road. To the south from 1886, following the death of the Hon. F.G.Molyneux of Earl's Court, the woods and fields behind Mount Ephraim were developed as Molyneux Park Road, Court Road and Earl's Road; and in 1891, Boyne House which had some 17 acres was sold and promptly demolished to create Boyne Park, Somerville Gardens, Mayfield Road and Oakdale Road.

It was therefore almost inevitable that when the Trustees failed to sell Great Culverden as a whole, it would be split up. In 1927, Great Culverden was demolished and the estate divided into lots which were put up for auction.

At this second auction, one of the principal bidders was the Tunbridge Wells Hospital Committee, who bought the 11 acres which fronted onto Mount Ephraim. The existing hospital in Grosvenor Road had become too small for the expanding population and the new site was considered ideal. However it was to be almost four years before the

The Duchess of York (later the Queen Mother) laying the Foundation Stone of the new Hospital, July 1932.

foundation stone was laid by HRH The Duchess of York (later to be Queen Elizabeth, the Queen Mother) on 19th. July 1932; and almost six years before the new Kent & Sussex Hospital, which had been built at a cost of £150,000, was formally declared open in July 1934 by the Marchioness Camden.

The remaining 63 acres were bought for £25,858 by Culverden Chase Ltd, a company which had been formed by Col. John Egginton and Charles Hillman of the Baltic Saw Mills with the specific intention of buying and selling the land.

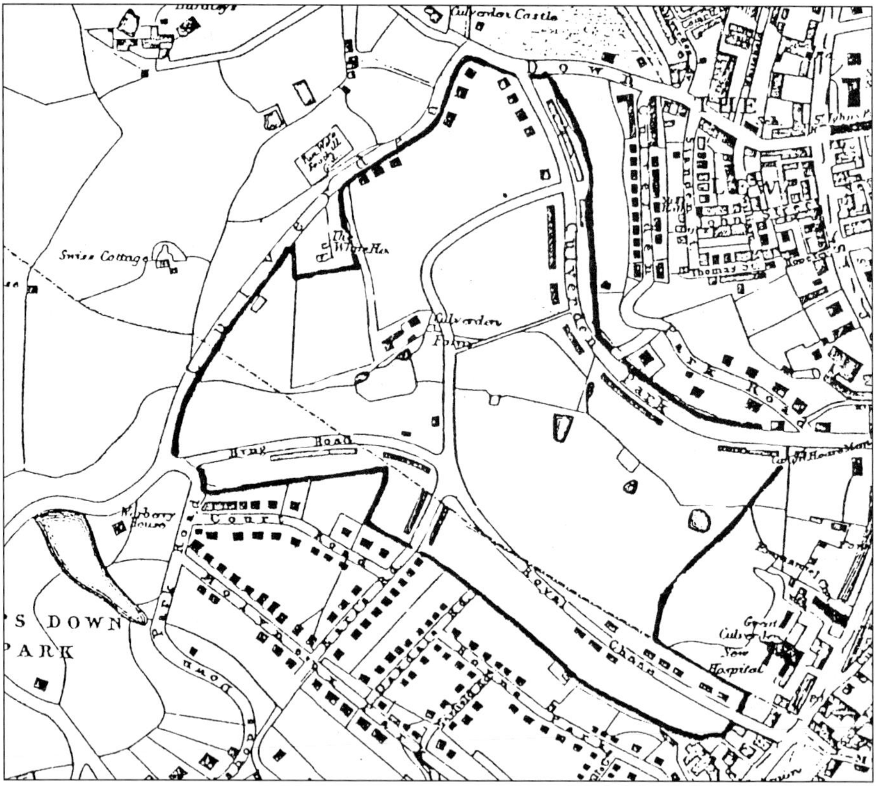

63 acres of land purchased by Culverden Chase Ltd, outlined in black.

Mr.Egginton (as he was then) had moved to Tunbridge Wells about 1900. When the developers of the Opera House and the Monson Road shops had run into financial difficulties in 1901, he provided the money to complete them and became manager of the theatre. He also founded the Autocar, the first bus service in Tunbridge Wells.

The Company now owned the Park, the nursery gardens, Culverden Farm and Buckingham House on Mount Ephraim. But there were problems of access since the Hospital site blocked access to the land behind. To gain access from the south-west, the Company demolished Buckingham House to make an entry for Royal Chase from Mount Ephraim.

The developments in Culverden Park sold quickly, possibly because it was an existing road. Twelve houses had been sold by 1931 and 42 by 1936. But Royal Chase was a much slower seller, possibly because it was a new road. Only five houses had been sold by 1931 and only 12 had been built by 1936. Royal Chase was not to be completed until the 1950s, long after Culverden Chase Ltd. had disappeared.

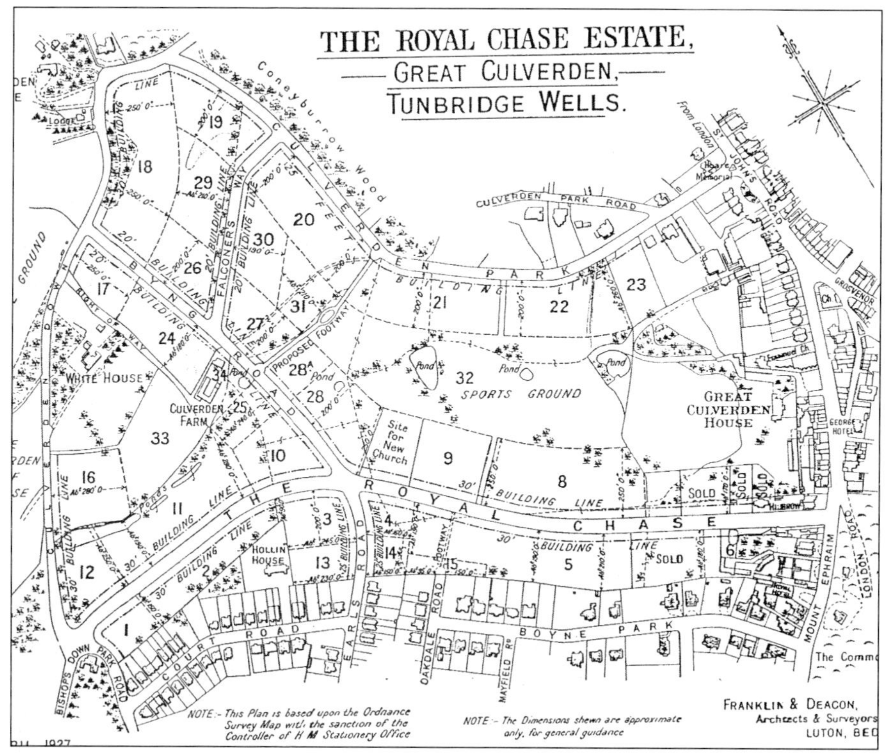

1927 Plan.

The Company started to be concerned about the slowness of developing the estate and sold off some land to other developers, who were equally unsuccessful since it did not become Knightsbridge Close until the 1960s. The Company also offered to sell land to Tunbridge Wells Borough Council, but they refused as they lacked the resources for development.

It was at this point that John Pownall, who lived in Green Shutters, Connaught Way (one of then only five houses in this new road) and who was unaware of the Company's offer to the Council, came up with the idea that residents might wish to buy some land and preserve it as an open space for their own enjoyment. The land in question was the 'Park', the valley immediately behind the Kent & Sussex site, which was less suitable for development since it would have needed considerable expenditure to drain and prepare for building.

He approached the Company, who said that they might be prepared to sell the 9½ acres (which they knew would be the last to be developed

Aerial view looking west over Kent & Sussex Hospital and Great Culverden Park. Note: Emmanuel Church and spire, bottom RH corner. Photo c.1934.

because of the topography) for £1,500. He then approached his neighbours, finding invaluable support from Donald Stoakes, an Estate Agent, of 19 Culverden Park. Contemporary records highlight the frustration and irritation of those involved in achieving their goal, but in reality they achieved results very quickly by today's standards. The first meeting of householders took place on 28th. April 1936 and the Conveyance and Trust Deed was signed on 5th. December 1936, a mere seven months later.

Until this time, the Park had no name, being referred to as ''The Park', 'the Pleasure Ground' or 'the said land'. It was proposed that it should be called 'The Royal Chase Park', but since the majority of 'Freeholders' (at that time) lived in Culverden Park, it was not acceptable. In the light of history, they settled for 'Great Culverden' for the land and 'Great Culverden Park' for the title.

The original legal agreement made in 1936 gave the rights in the Park to those owners who had subscribed to its purchase. Ownership of a share in the Park has subsequently been made available to all households backing onto the Park.

Soon afterwards, the Second World War intervened.

At 5.10 pm on 12th. September, 1940, a lone German bomber, probably on its way from (or maybe still on its way to) London, off-loaded a stick of bombs (22 small bombs, one of which failed to explode; and 30 incendiaries) across Tunbridge Wells in a path stretching from Connaught Way to the Park, to the Hospital, and the remainder down the hill on the shopping area. Casualties were 12 killed, 15 injured and 95 properties damaged. It was probably the worst attack that Tunbridge Wells was to experience in the War.

For Great Culverden Park, it was ironic that the first bomb hit Green Shutters in Connaught Way, the home of the Pownalls, reducing it to rubble. Fortunately all the family was away, so there were no casualties.

The nature of the Park has changed in the past 70 years. What was largely open pasture has turned into mostly woodland, much as Tunbridge Wells Common did in the 20th. century, due to grazing ceasing and to lack of maintenance particularly during the Second World War and just after. It is now the deliberate policy of the Park management to preserve it as woodland with its native trees, flowers and wildlife, but in a planned and controlled manner.

CHAPTER 10

WHAT HAPPENED TO THE RESIDENTIAL PARK?

by John Cunningham

This monograph has traced the progress of the residential park from the early 19th. century and in particular the development of the residential parks of Royal Tunbridge Wells. Tunbridge Wells, due to the presence of Decimus Burton, had in many ways led the way. Other towns followed, particularly newer 'spa' towns with a similar upper-middle class population such as Cheltenham, Harrogate and Leamington.

We have seen that in its origins the residential park was based on ideas of 'rus in urbe' for the richer urban family, but that it changed in style and size over time, as its appeal became more widespread across middle and lower middle-classes. Cost was obviously a major consideration in this change and as the concept filtered down to the less wealthy, its scope was inevitably curtailed as they 'cut their coat according to their cloth' and developed smaller properties on smaller sites. But the idealised concept of Arcadian back-to-nature and green pastures, had become well-established and remained with all classes, however small the property.

Without doubt it has been a major influence on the whole of British society and it has contributed significantly to the British love of gardens and gardening. It is a plausible explanation why gardens and gardening are a major, if not the major pastime for the British, probably more so than for any other nation.

It also influenced the creation of public parks. Since 1703, Tunbridge Wells had had The Grove which can possibly claim to be Britain's first public park. But the municipal parks so beloved of the Victorians did not begin until 1843, when Birkenhead Council bought land to create the first publicly-funded park. Interestingly, this park had 125 acres for public use; and 60 acres for upper-middle class houses which skirted and overlooked the park – in effect a residential park. No doubt the latter paid for the former, however indirectly. It was designed by Joseph Paxton as an idealised vision of the countryside with two ornamental lakes and woodland; and it was to be used by the American Frederick Olmstead as the blue print for his 850-acre Central Park in New York in the 1850s.

But nothing stands still and everything changes over time. And so it was with Residential Parks. Architecture can rarely dictate living style; and generally living style dictates architecture. And so, as living style changes, so does architecture.

The concept of Residential Parks developed before the advent of the railways, or at least before railways had had a major impact on life, which was not until the 1850-1860s.

Railways however changed Britain in many ways:

- not only did they add a significant fillip to the scope, breadth and speed of the Industrial Revolution which had been underway since the mid-18th century;

- but they made population movement much more practical and much less expensive, so that the movement of population, from the countryside to the towns to service the employee requirements of the growing Industrial Revolution, became much easier;

- they were not the cause of, but they were a major influence on the development and extension of suburbs (which had of course had existed to some extent in major towns for at least 500 years). There is little doubt that suburbs were the major residential development of the second half of the 19th century, due principally to railways giving employees, particularly middle and lower-middle class ones, the chance to live much further away from their work, than previously. (It is worth noting that railways remained too expensive on a daily basis for the working classes until the Cheap Trains Act of 1864 created the Workman's Ticket, for travel before 7am.)

In the case of Tunbridge Wells, the railways also brought London much closer. While the stagecoach had been more expensive and took 4-5 hours to cover the 36 miles, the first trains were not only less expensive, but took only two hours until about 1870, and then improved to under an hour, which it remains to this day.

While the coming of the railway undoubtedly contributed to the population growth of Tunbridge Wells – the ten-yearly Censuses show that the population virtually trebled from 10,587 in 1851 to 29,296 in 1891 – nobody seemed to have realised at the time that this growth would not continue forever (and would indeed level out between 1911 and 1951, so that it was not to reach 40,000 until 1961 as the table on the following page shows).

Population of Tunbridge Wells

Year	No.	Increase/Decrease
1801	1,000 (est)	–
1831	5,929	4,929
1841	8,302	2,373
1851	10,587	2,285
1861	13,807	3,220
1871	19,410	5,603
1881	24,309	4,899
1891	29,296	4,987
1901	33,373	4,097
1911	35,568	–129
1931	35,367	–201
1941	No Census	
1951	38,397	3,030
1961	40,340	1,943

Source: OPCS National Census

It took time for developers in Tunbridge Wells to realise that there was a real decline in housing demand after 1891. This was disguised by the fact that, when the First World War came and property development came to a halt, the decline in demand was attributed to the War and not the lack of population growth.

The population of Tunbridge Wells remained static throughout the 1920s and 1930s no doubt due to the severe economic depression of the late 1920s and most of the 1930s. The coming of the Second World War in 1939 literally put Tunbridge Wells in the first line of defence, and there was little opportunity for population growth (and property development) until the 1950s.

But it was not just lack of population growth that was hindering property development in Tunbridge Wells in the first half of the 20th. century. Society and lifestyle was changing radically and this affected the type of property people wanted.

The First World War was the most important watershed for Britain in the social order, in lifestyle and in the nature of employment, particularly for women. The employment market in Britain ended the First World War with 743,702 fewer employees, since that was the number of British men who had been killed (Hansard, 9th. March 1923). During the four-year War, women had learnt to take the place of men in many industries and services; and that meant that there were at least three-quarters of a million women who did not need or want to take domestic service, when they could have better pay and/or more satisfying jobs, with more regular hours. Prior to the War, domestic service had been the only employment choice for most women. After the War, they had many more choices.

This had an obvious impact on the domestic employment market. With fewer staff available, it created a small but nonetheless inflationary increase in wages, which in turn led to lower levels of domestic staff employment – a vicious circle (or even a downward spiral). It meant that if you already had a large house (and grounds), you became increasingly aware that you did not have enough help to run it (even if you could afford to pay for it).

The problem became progressively more acute in the late 1920s and 1930s, despite the Depression; and the only solution, in the absence of sufficient staff, was either to keep on and let everything – house, grounds – deteriorate slowly, often so slowly that you might not realise that it was happening; or move to smaller, more manageable properties, which is what those without previous commitments were already doing.

There was a clear trend in the late 1920s and 1930s towards to smaller, more manageable houses and gardens, which could be run with little or no domestic help. This led over the next 30-40 years to three developments:

- large(r) houses being divided into flats;
- large(r) houses being demolished to allow more, smaller houses/flats;
- large(r) plots (i.e. particularly gardens) being sub-divided to accommodate by in-filling the site, more houses/flats.

Sometimes all three developments could occur on the same site, as many sites in Tunbridge Wells can demonstrate. However for the major Parks in Tunbridge Wells, while they had division and sub-division, they were generally spared demolition, since the quality of their architecture was recognised and they were frequently listed for protection.

The division/sub-division/demolition trend was prevalent throughout the late 1940s, the 1950s, the 1960s and also well into the 1970s. But in the 1970s, there emerged a new trend (funded/afforded by greater personal prosperity and a greater interest in the past) which was against demolition and in favour of renovation and restoration; and this has lead to many sub-divided houses being restored to single occupancy. So there has been a distinct movement towards renovation and restoration, and against demolition. (It was also realised, but somewhat belatedly, by the developers that renovation/restoration was also generally cheaper, and more popular with public opinion, than demolition.)

The net result of all this is that the Residential Park which could have vanished as uneconomic in a strictly commercial development world, is now a 'protected species'. It has evolved over time and there are a number of varieties of Parks, reflecting both horizontal development over time, and vertical development through penetration of the social classes.

Its place in architectural history is, we hope, assured. The subject deserves much deeper research and analysis and we hope that what has been written in this brief monograph is sufficient to lead to further publications in more depth.

Crocodile Lodge, Camden Park.

NOTES, REFERENCES AND BIBLIOGRAPHY

In general, the following locations are prime depositaries for material in this monograph:

Tunbridge Wells Reference Library
Tunbridge Wells Museum
Centre for Kentish Studies (CKS) at Maidstone
East Sussex Records Office (ESRO) at Lewes

For most chapters, the following are specific sources. Consequently, they are *generally* not repeated in the individual Chapter listings below:

Maps: Bowra, 1738; Billings (Britton) 1832; Stidolph, 1838; Colbran 1839, 1845 & 1851; Gisborne, 1849; Clifford, 1855; Brackett 1868
Ordnance Survey maps, 1867, 1897, 1909 and 1938
Population Censuses: 1851, 1861, 1871, 1881, 1891, 1901
Tunbridge Wells Planning Applications Index 1867-1891; 1891-1913
Kelly's Kent Directory – various dates
Kelly's Directories for Tunbridge Wells – various dates
Kent & Sussex (Tunbridge Wells) Courier – various dates
Pelton's Guides and Directories – various dates
Sale catalogues (held in Reference Library)
Susan Brown: Researching Tunbridge Wells, RTWCS LHG 2003
Roger Farthing: History of Mount Sion, Phillimore, 2003
Royal Tunbridge Wells, Phillimore, 1990
Nikolaus Pevsner: The Buildings of England: West Kent and the Weald by John Newman: 2nd. Edition: Penguin Books 1976
Alan Savidge: Royal Tunbridge Wells [1st edition] 1975

Chapter 1

Mark Girouard: Life in the English Country House. A Social and Architectural History. Yale University Press, 1978
Ann Saunders: The Art and Architecture of London. Phaidon, 1984
Ben Weinreb & Christopher Hibbert : The London Encyclopaedia. Macmillan. 1983
Bob Stanley: Birkenhead Park: The Times, 12th October, 2004.

Chapter 2

1. Hussey,C., Calverley Park, Tunbridge Wells – Country Life, 8.5.1969 and 1.5.1969
2. Farthing, R., A History of Mount Sion, 2003, p.11

3. Colbran, J., New Guide for Tunbridge Wells, 1840, p.30
4. Ibid.p.33
5. The Tunbridge Wells Visitor. Vol 3, No.1 , 5.7. 1834, p.15
6. Clifford's Visitor's Guide for Tunbridge Wells, 1853, p.40
7. The Tunbridge Wells Visitor, Vol.3, No.17, 18.10.1834, p.254

Chapter 3

Abergavenny Archives, ESRO – Estate Correspondence
Colbran's Tunbridge Wells Guide 1840
Nevill Estates Survey, 1899, ESRO
Nevill Court Estate Plan, 1930
Rusthall Manor Archives – Correspondence
Sale Catalogues
Speldhurst Tithe map 1840
Terence Davies: 'Tunbridge Wells. The Gentle Aspect.' Phillimore, 1976

Chapter 4

Camden Archives, CKS
Colbran's Directory 1847
Sale Catalogues

Chapter 5

Valuation Office Records: 'New Domesday Survey' 1910-1915. PRO
Vera Coomber :William Barnsley Hughes, Architect of Victorian Tunbridge Wells. RTWCS Newsletter, Spring and Summer 1994
Sale Catalogues

Chapter 6

1. Kent and Sussex Courier 23.6.1882
2. "Woodbury Park and St.Johns Area Walks". RTWCS, 1983
3. Clifton Cottage sales catalogue, 1890
4. Article on Edwards Family in Tunbridge Wells Family History Society Journal No.21, October 2001 pp.13-17.
5. Farthing, Roger " Royal Tunbridge Wells" – research notes deposited with Tunbridge Wells Reference Library

Chapter 7

Tunbridge Wells Planning Applications Index 1867-1891; 1891-1913
Return of Owners of Land, Kent, 1873, revised 1877 and Vol.1 (Kent) 1875
Vera Coomber:William Barnsley Hughes, Architect of Victorian Tunbridge Wells. RTWCS Newsletter, Spring and Summer 1994

Kelsall Lodge Public Inquiry: RTWCS Newsletter, February 1979
Keith Hetherington: 'High Brooms and its Brickworks'. Bygone Kent Vol.15 no.8 (August 1994)
Dora Ware: Short Dictionary of British Architects (1967)

Chapter 8

Abergavenny Estate Archives, ESRO: accounts, correspondence, plans and maps.
1881 census RG11;1891 census RG12; 1901 census RG13.
Tunbridge Wells Borough Council Archives: Beale's plans, Strange's plans

Lorna and Brian Bailey	Nonconformist Churches in Tunbridge Wells
Peter Beale	Beale and Sons Builders, 2003
Susan Brown	Town development file
Geoffrey Copus	RTWCS Walks no. 8
John Cunningham	The Origins of Warwick Park, 2001
John Cunningham	The Nevill Ground and Cricket in Tunbridge Wells, 2003

Chapter 9

Peter Watson: A History of Great Culverden Park. Illustrated by Penny Mitchell: June 1983: typescript.
Souvenir Brochure produced by John Jarvis Ltd., commemorating the Opening of the Kent & Sussex Hospital, July 1934
Brochure : A Garden Home in the Garden of England – The Culverden Chase Estate. Courier Printing & Publishing Co. 1927

Chapter 10

OPCS : United Kingdom National Censuses
Hansard, 1923

NOTES ON THE AUTHORS

Ann Bates was born and has lived all her life in Tunbridge Wells. After leaving Blackheath High School, she studied Art at the Tunbridge Wells School of Art and in London at the Central School of Arts and Crafts (now St. Martin's Central School). She worked as a florist and after retiring, has researched local and family history. She is a granddaughter of Thomas Bates (1864-1930), who built many houses in Warwick Park, and Roedean, Blatchington and Forest Roads at the beginning of the 20th. century.

Susan Brown is the Community Librarian responsible for Local Studies at Tunbridge Wells Library. She studied Library Science at the Brighton College of Technology (now Brighton University) and qualified as a Chartered Librarian. Since then she has worked in the local library service in a number of capacities. She has lived in Tunbridge Wells since childhood; and knows and loves the town and its history very much. She is the compiler of the Group's second monograph *'Researching Royal Tunbridge Wells. A bibliography of historical sources'.*

Geoffrey and Brenda Copus have lived in Tunbridge Wells since 1960. Brenda was a professional record agent and genealogist for many years, while Geoffrey's main interest in the area is the history of the church and parish of St. Barnabas. They both collaborated with the late Roger Farthing in cataloguing the extensive residual archives of the Manor of Rusthall before these were deposited at the Centre for Kentish Studies.

John Cunningham read History at Peterhouse, Cambridge and has written several local histories, including ' The Origins of Warwick Park'. His career was essentially in Marketing in the advertising, market research and publishing industries. Now retired, he is Vice-Chairman of the Royal Tunbridge Wells Civic Society and Hon. Secretary of its Local History Group.

Dr. Philip Whitbourn OBE, FSA, FRIBA is a qualified architect who, before retirement, held the post of Chief Architect at English Heritage and then the post of Secretary to the International Council on Monuments and Sites. Now retired, he is President of the Royal Tunbridge Wells Civic Society, of which he was a founder member in 1959. He is Chairman of the Local History Group of the Society and author of the Group's first monograph entitled *'Decimus Burton. Architect and Gentleman.'* He is also part-author with Cecil Beeby of the Group's third monograph entitled *'The Skinners' School. Its controversial birth and its landmark buildings.'*

INDEX

D

E

F

G

William Nevill, KG, 1st Marquess and 5th Earl of Abergavenny and 19th Baron Bergavenny (1826-1915), in 1897.

Sealink Memories

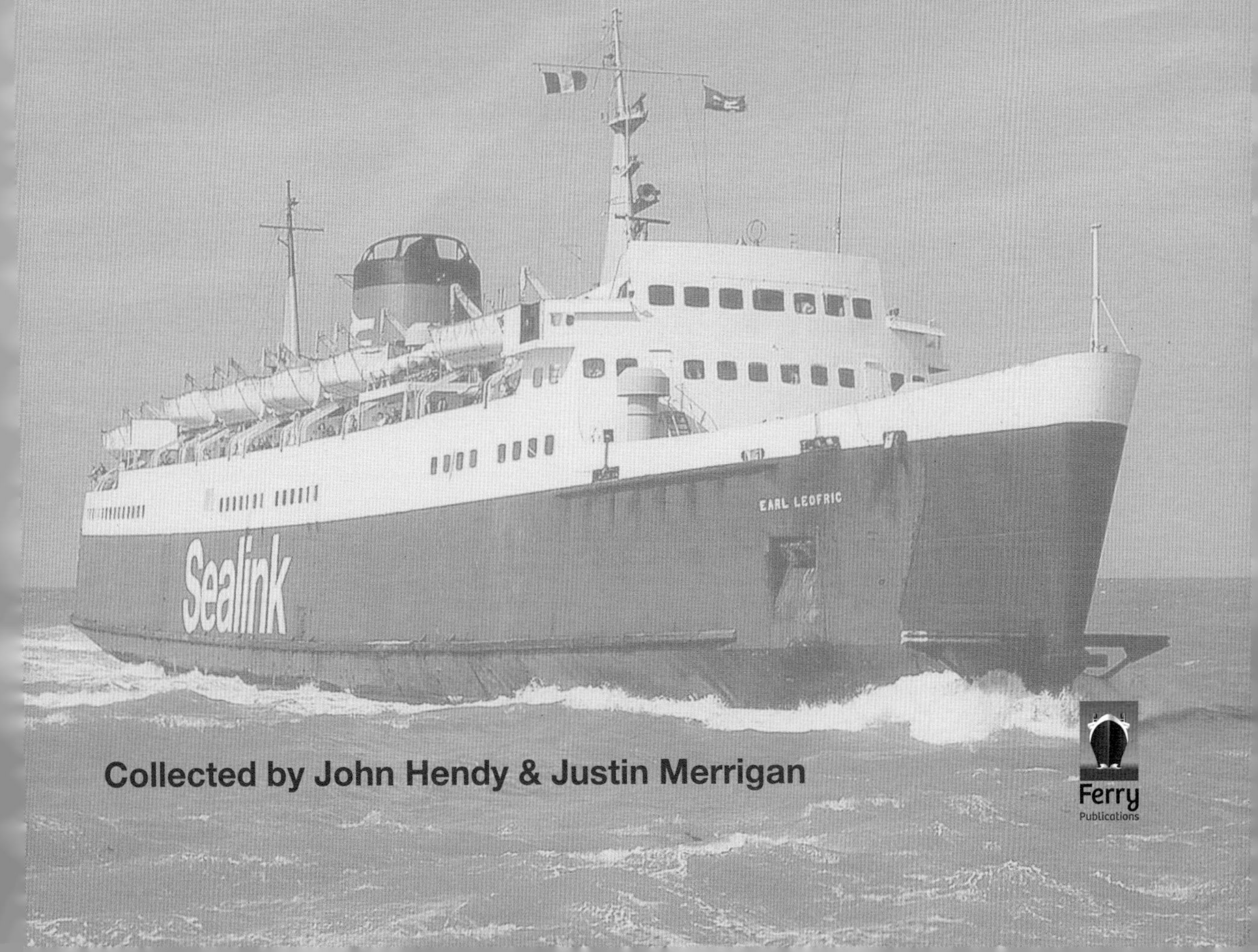

Collected by John Hendy & Justin Merrigan

First published in the Isle of Man in 2011
by
Ferry Publications
PO Box 33
Ramsey
Isle of Man
IM99 4LP

ISBN 978-1-906608-42-2

Produced in the Isle of Man by Lily Publications Ltd. Ferry Publications is a trading name of Lily Publications Ltd.

Introduction

It is amazing to consider that Sealink UK Ltd – the former railway-owned nationalised ferry company – ceased to exist as long ago as 1984 and yet there are many who still remember the operator with affection and nostalgia.

The railway systems in the UK were brought under Government control in 1948 and the shipping arms of the 'Big Four' (the London & North Eastern Railway, London Midland & Scottish Railway, Great Western Railway and the Southern Railway) were absorbed into regional organisations which by and large carried on just as they did previously. It was not until some 20 years later that the marine sections were together grouped under a central management to form British Railways (Shipping & International Services Division) which in 1970 began trading as Sealink.

However, old habits certainly died hard and each of the traditional railway ports largely retained its unique identity, vessel requirements and approach to ship handling so that changes within the unified fleet were inevitably slow to occur. Changing traffic demands and the move to multi-purpose vessels gradually saw the phasing out of passenger only ships (the Mail Boats of happy memory), steam-powered ships and then stern-loading car ferries unable to accommodate high-sided freight lorries.

With the formation of Sealink UK Ltd in 1979, the company's in-house naval architects (Tony Rogan and Don Ripley) now produced ships which were capable of operating on more than one route as 'inter-availability' became the norm. Until that time, ships had tended to have been built for the routes on which they served for their entire careers and problems frequently occurred later on if and when they were required to switch ports. New ships, mainly of Scandinavian heritage, were frequently chartered and found wanting although some impressed and were retained for longer periods.

The Sealink fleet will be remembered as an eclectic collection of traditional ships, mostly produced by British shipbuilders for the 'Big Four' railway companies and their regional successors, many of which survived into an age to which they did not belong and struggled to compete against a variety of new operators using modern tonnage and aggressive marketing techniques. The fleet was always hampered by a lack of investment and as time progressed, it found it increasingly difficult to cope with the changing demands of the industry.

Sealink's last quartet of cross-Channel ships were built at Harland & Wolff's Belfast yard in 1980-81 and the final one, the former *St David* survived in service across the North Channel as the *Stena Caledonia* until 2011 – the very last large Sealink ship in operation in home waters. Post-nationalisation, much new tonnage was promised by Sea Containers but this sadly failed to materialise. When Sealink British Ferries was swallowed up by a ravenous Stena Line in 1990, the renamed Sealink Stena Line and then Stena Sealink Line inevitably became simply Stena Line in 1996 when the end of an era was finally realised.

Almost all the ships that are mentioned here have long since gone from these shores and the name Sealink has passed into history. The contributions contained within these pages serve to capture something of the company's unique identity from those who worked in the ships and knew their quirks and characteristics like no others.

As many of Sealink UK's Masters recall with fondness those early pre-Sealink steamers in which they joined as junior officers, we have also included those as they were very much the foundation upon which Sealink was operated.

These memories serve to capture a bygone era in the annals of British short-sea shipping and we are delighted to have the opportunity of sharing them with a new and appreciative audience. Many show light-hearted and amusing incidents encountered in everyday service whilst others serve to illustrate the demands of the ferry industry, navigating increasingly larger ships into harbours built by the Victorians for an entirely different type of trade. What shines through is the high levels of professionalism and seamanship shown by these men. To many, theirs was just another job; to them it was a way of life.

John Hendy, Kent — Justin Merrigan, Tasmania

Preface

Even for those of us who once worked for the shipping arm of British Rail, the Sealink brand is now a distant memory of which a whole new generation of seafarers now working in the ferry industry know little or nothing. It is therefore perhaps not surprising that they often refer to those of us dating from that era as the 'Railway Children'. Be that as it may, for many of us these were happy days when hard work within a very professional marine environment was at times lightened by amusing incidents and good fun plus a sprinkling of notable characters.

Coming from careers with some of the United Kingdom's many deep sea shipping companies, I suspect that most of us opting for a move to the railway ships did so to have more time at home expecting the price to be a sort of boring, less challenging and fairly hum drum sort of life with little variety. How wrong we were! It was certainly different, but infinitely varied, always posing challenges and consistently at a fast pace.

In addition to this dwindling band of 'mature' seafarers and port staff who survive in the industry from the Sealink years, there is, remarkably, one of the Company's former cross-Channel ships still in British waters and performing the sort of service for which she was built just over 30 years ago. This is the 12,619 gross ton *Stena Caledonia* which came into service on 10th August 1981 as the *St David*, the last of four 'Saint' Class vessels built for British Rail's Sealink UK Ltd at the Belfast yard of Harland & Wolff.

Having first served on the ship in 1982, I well recall the latter years of BR and as she is about to be displaced by more modern and larger ships this is perhaps a good time to draw together some of those Sealink Memories and I congratulate Justin Merrigan and John Hendy for doing so.

Capt. J. M. Paterson,
Senior Master, *Stena Caledonia*

Captain Murray Paterson, Senior Master, *Stena Caledonia*. (Scott Mackey)

Looking aft from the *Avalon*'s flying bridge. (Kenneth Whyte)

Contents

The *St David* arrives at Holyhead on completion of her delivery voyage from Belfast under the command of Captain Idwal Pritchard: 5th August 1981.
(John Marsh)

▲ The *Galloway Princess* arrives at Stranraer's Ross Pier. (Kenneth Whyte)

▶ The *Antrim Princess* alongside at Larne with P&O's *Puma* arriving from Fleetwood. (Kenneth Whyte)

Stranraer

THE LAST PRINCESS

Captain Hamish Ross

Following the tragic loss of the *Princess Victoria* in January 1953 the Stranraer-Larne route entered a period of uncertainty, with at times, even rumours of possible closure. The turn round, when it came, was driven by the introduction in 1961 of possibly the most beautiful ship to ever serve the route, the Denny-built *Caledonian Princess*. Her arrival and almost immediate positive impact was to build a platform for future expansion.

Traffic began to build up and although in the short term chartering in various vessels catered for extra capacity at peak times, it was announced in 1965 that a new ship was to be built to join the *Caledonian Princess*. In the meantime, in 1966 the *Stena Nordica* was chartered from Stena Line of Sweden to help meet demand. The new *Antrim Princess* duly arrived in 1967. Built by Hawthorn Leslie on the Tyne she was British Rail's first ever 'drive through' ro-ro ferry. The growth of traffic, especially freight, continued apace and the charter of the Atlantic Steam Navigation's *Baltic Ferry* further boosted freight capacity on the route in May 1970.

Meanwhile, the exciting news was that a sister ship to the *Antrim Princess* had been ordered and would be built in Venice. In 1971 the dramatic growth of the route in all sectors of traffic was confirmed by the arrival in June 1971 of the freight ship *Stena Trailer* on charter from Stena Line. Renamed the *Dalriada* she was followed by the new *Ailsa Princess* in July, releasing the *Caledonian Princess* for the Fishguard station.

The year 1973 saw the introduction of a competing service to Stranraer when the Atlantic Steam Navigation (part of the European Ferries Group) opened up a Cairnryan to Larne service. Fears that such a service would badly damage the Sealink operation proved unfounded. In fact, the combined frequency of sailings to Larne by the two operators acted as a magnet, especially to the road haulage operators. Hauliers from Eire and Northern Ireland chose in growing numbers to 'go over the top' as they called it.

The Sealink fleet on the route was further strengthened in 1974 by the acquisition of the *Dalriada*'s younger sister, the *Stena Carrier*, which joined us as the *Ulidia*. The fortunes of this famous route had swung dramatically in just over a decade since the introduction of the *Caledonian Princess*. But it was now becoming clear that the era of ships such as the 'Antrim' and 'Ailsa' was fast passing and that larger vessels with much greater freight capacity were needed to gain the necessary economies of scale. In 1977 it was decided to replace the *Dalriada* by chartering the new and much larger *Stena Topper* (renamed *Darnia*) built in Austria, but it was also announced that a large new ship was to be built for the route. This was dramatic and exciting news!

Double tier linkspans were to be built at Larne (by Larne Harbour Ltd) and Stranraer to cope efficiently with this new tonnage, whilst still maintaining fast port turn round times and thus frequency of sailings. This required substantial investment at Stranraer – a new berth, Ross Pier, with a double tier linkspan was built, a deeper channel marked by beacons was dredged and land reclaimed from Loch Ryan to increase freight marshalling facilities.

The highly respected Sealink in-house Naval Architects Tony Rogan and Don Ripley had been working for some considerable time on a new design of ro-ro vessel which could load and discharge from two decks simultaneously at the double tier linkspans, but would also have the facility to operate effectively at ports with only a single tier linkspan. This was to be a standard design which would make these ships interchangeable between the various Sealink ports. Four of these ships were ordered from the famous Harland & Wolff shipyard in Belfast and they became known as the 'Saint Class'. Actually three became Saints, but the Stranraer ship became a princess – the *Galloway Princess*.

I remember in the build-up to the order for these ships, Tony Rogan and Don Ripley fully consulting with the on-board and shore teams. As an example the three 'Saints' were to be fitted with bow rudders, but at Stranraer we asked instead that a bulbous be fitted to our ship; this achieved significant economy of power. The prospect of this new 'Princess' created great excitement both within the fleet and at both ports.

The *Darnia* was meanwhile modified to make her fully compatible with the double tier linkspan operation. The *Galloway Princess* was launched without ceremony in May 1979 and I remember being present with Tony Rogan, Fergus Gibson (General Manager, Sealink Scotland) and a few others as she took to the water for the first time. Unfortunately, delays in fitting out meant that she did not undergo sea trials until March 1980. She was eventually named with due pomp and ceremony at Belfast by Mrs Joan Soane, wife of Leslie Soane, General Manager of British Rail (Scotland), who was also Chairman of Sealink Scotland. The new vessel was shown off at various PR events including a trip up the Clyde to Glasgow and received tremendous and very positive media coverage.

She of course received a tremendous welcome in her home port of Stranraer, with many people, myself included, being struck by her immense size in comparison to the 'Antrim' and the 'Ailsa'. Now she would be small against some of the giant ferries of today, but she perhaps gave us a taste of what was to come. Undoubtedly, the arrival of the *Darnia* and the *Galloway Princess* took this historic route to a new level, giving Sealink Scotland a commanding market share lead in all traffic sectors over its immediate Loch Ryan competitor.

The *Galloway Princess* was to be the last 'Princess' on the famous short-sea route between Scotland and Northern Ireland, being renamed *Stena Galloway* following Stena Line's acquisition of Sealink. The Saint class ships have proved over three decades to be fine and adaptable vessels that have operated successfully on many different routes and with various owners. Their fine record stands as a tribute to the Sealink naval architects led by Tony Rogan and Don Ripley who were behind their creative design.

DIVE! DIVE! DIVE!

Captain David Bark

The *Holyhead Ferry I* was a fairly regular visitor to the Stranraer-Larne route to relieve the *Caledonian Princess* for annual overhaul and refit. Although pilotage was not compulsory in either Loch Ryan or Larne Harbour, it was the practice to place a Mate on board to act as Pilot/liaison officer and on this occasion it was myself who was selected for this task.

One evening we were bound for Larne in bad weather. The Welsh Master, Captain Len Evans, had reduced speed slightly to ease the motion of the ship in the heavy seas and had gone below momentarily leaving me on the bridge with the watchkeeping officer. There had been a few distress messages, not unusual in these conditions, but nothing in our area.

Despite the weather, visibility was excellent under a bright moon, when the bridge wing lookout reported seeing "masts in the water" on the port bow. Grabbing the 7x50s (binoculars), I followed him out to the bridge wing and right enough there they were, two masts sticking out of the sea, swaying about, maybe three miles away. A sinking fishing boat!

I ordered a course change to close with them, rang standby on the telegraphs and called the Master. After a while we realised they must have been further away than we first thought, because we didn't seem to be closing. We increased speed, plunging through the heavy seas to the rescue,

The *Holyhead Ferry 1*.
(Robert Matheson)

spray lashing the bridge wings. We still didn't seem to be getting any closer, in fact, if anything they were getting away from us.

Then realisation dawned; another look through the 7x50s. Not masts… periscopes!

A NICE QUIET PINT

Captain David Bark

A nice quiet Sunday evening in Stranraer. The *Antrim Princess* was tied up to the east side of the Railway Pier out of the way of other ferry traffic, the harbour watches had been set and night orders written. It was time for the off duty Mate to go ashore for a quiet pint in the North West Castle before bed.

In those days the Castle Bar was entered from the front of the hotel; it was secluded, sheltered and very quiet. So quiet, that very often one wouldn't hear the wind rising, as on that evening it did. From out of nowhere a storm shrieked across Loch Ryan, a Westerly gale accompanied by driving rain that shook the *Antrim Princess* and one by one carried away her moorings until the duty crew on board managed to stabilise her with extra lines until it was impossible to put any more out.

The ship lay shuddering in the gusts about 30 feet away from the quayside, her gangway hanging down from the sally port door where it had been dragged off the pier. The duty 2nd Mate and the 3rd Engineer had the bow thrust and main engines running to take some strain off the moorings. They could do nothing more now until the wind abated.

The shore gang changed shifts and one of the lads going off duty called into the Castle Bar for a drink on his way home. As the off duty Mate sitting alone at a table raised his foaming tankard to his lips, he managed to overhear the brief conversation… "Gimme a half please George", the dripping customer shook the rain from his hat, "Bloody 'Antrim'." At the sound of his ship's name, the Mate paused in the act of sipping from his pint. The barman placed a glass of whiskey in front of the wet customer and rang up the

The *Antrim Princess* 'out of the way' at Stranraer as the *Ailsa Princess* loads for Larne. (Kenneth Whyte)

purchase on the till, "Why, what's wrong with her?" A gulp of whiskey, "She only parted all her moorings, didn't she?"

The front door banged shut; the barman and his customer looked towards the empty table and the hardly touched pint. "I wonder why he's in such a hurry?"

SEALINK DAYS

Captain Murray Paterson

When I joined Sealink in April 1980 I was appointed to the *Ailsa Princess,* one of the Mail Ships then operating between Stranraer and Larne. Just a few weeks later I was on watch on a beautiful bright and flat calm day when with the ship at full speed I saw something in the water some distance ahead. Close examination with binoculars was at first inconclusive, then to my horror it began to look as if the object was a body. Startled and unsure I hesitated, not sure about calling the Master or about slowing down, but I did alter course slightly in order that the object would pass down our starboard side.

Never has dithering or lack of confidence served me so well for the object was in fact an inflatable woman and I dread to think the notoriety I would have acquired had I been bolder and instigated a rescue.

During the 1970s the Stranraer-Larne service was busy and expanding with the result that there was a succession of chartered vessels brought to the route to help cope with the traffic. On one German freight ship the Captain had noticed that every time they passed close to Cairn Ryan Point in Loch Ryan a fleeting glimpse could be had of a grand turreted house at the end of a tree-lined driveway. "What sort of person would live in such a fine place?" he asked of the local Sealink liaison Master. "The sort of person who would sink the *Bismark*" came the reply as this was the family home of Admiral Sir Frederick Dalrymple-Hamilton who had been Captain of HMS *Rodney*, one of the battleships responsible for the demise of the enemy vessel.

The 'Troubles', as the past problems of Northern Ireland are often called, were a dark chapter in the history of the Province, but even here the occasional lighter moment could be discerned.

At one point the leaders of the Loyalist community called a general strike which on the day paralysed commerce and transport links to and from Ulster. While made idle by the strike, the Captain and mate of one Sealink vessel caught in Larne decided to take advantage of this rare chance and take a walk into town. On the way, there is a steep road bridge over the railway and here they were suddenly confronted by a barricade presided over by a number of masked men. Somewhat taken aback and uncertain as to the best (safest) course of action, the two men decided it might be best to continue and as they approached the roadblock and passed through a gap which had been made for them there was a chorus of "evening Cap'n" from the several Larne dockers who were manning the obstruction.

One of the sadder duties we perform from time to time is to carry families escorting the remains of a loved one on their last journey. We always try to give these families special consideration by allowing them to board separately and have, when possible, an area to themselves. Most of the time this involves groups going to Northern Ireland but just occasionally it is people heading in the other direction.

While serving on the *Antrim Princess* we had one such group coming out of Larne. The relatives were taken to the accommodation and the coffin to a locker on the car deck from where it would be collected by a hearse at the end of the crossing. After the discharge of cargo at Stranraer, word came that the family had asked if it would be possible to have a few quiet minutes alone with the coffin before the hearse arrived.

This unusual request caused me some concern as I knew that one side of the locker used for coffins was where the ship's carpenters stored plumbing spares of all sorts. Asking for a few minutes to check if this was possible, I immediately fled downstairs to the passenger cabins below the car deck and was much relieved to find one unlocked. Stripping off the sheets from the bunk I draped them over the offending ballcocks etc. Dignity maintained – I hope!

Not everyone enjoys refit. It can mean long hours of hard work in cold and indifferent weather conditions but it is also interesting, challenging and ultimately satisfying. In addition to carrying out the carefully planned programme of repairs and survey work, it is not at all uncommon to find unexpected matters which have to be dealt with. During one docking, the Master's toilet on the *Stena Galloway* (ex *Galloway Princess*) was being refurbished and when the cement screed and tiles covering the deck were removed it revealed some serious corrosion of the steelwork below. The Senior Chief Engineer at this time was a man of strong departmental loyalty who on seeing the damage was heard to comment in tones of resigned disappointment directed at Masters in general, "Is it any wonder that they miss the piers when they cannot even hit the toilet."

THE LAST OF THE LINE

Having previously sailed on the *Galloway Princess*, the first of the quartet of 'Saint' Class vessels introduced by Sealink for their English Channel and Irish

Sea services, it was 1982 when I came to know the *St David*, the last of the class. She came to the Stranraer-Larne route after a serious switchboard fire had disabled the *Antrim Princess* outside Larne harbour in foul weather, almost causing her loss.

The *St David* was an instant hit with our customers who enjoyed the spacious and uncomplicated vehicle decks and high standard of her lounges while the more elevated bridge was much appreciated by watchkeepers and the extra power (in comparison to the 'Galloway') very popular with the Masters when conditions were challenging. For the ratings more used to the dingy windowless accommodation below the vehicle decks of the old Mail Boats, the transition to cabins with a view high up in the hull was by comparison quite literally night and day.

The launch of the *St David* at Harland & Wolff: 25th September 1980. (Robert Anderson)

I recall Captain Hamish Ross, the Stranraer Ship & Port Manager visiting the bridge and suggesting to him that he should hang on to the ship. He in turn said that the route could not really afford the daily charter costs (she was a Holyhead ship), however, after doing refit relief with us during 1983 and 1984, she eventually was transferred and by that time her size and capacity were less of a luxury and more of a necessity.

Ever popular with those who sailed on her, the *St David* became the *Stena Caledonia* during the 1990 refit in a choice of name which reflected not only the change in ownership but a reminder of a previously successful northern corridor vessel – *Caledonian Princess*.

By 1991 the *Stena Caledonia* and the now *Stena Galloway* were joined by the *Stena Antrim* (ex *St Christopher*) and together ran the last years of the Larne service before transferring to the new Stranraer/Belfast route at the end of 1995. From time to time the fourth member of the 'Saints', *Stena Cambria* (ex *St Anselm*), came to act as relief ship.

The transition was another challenge to ship's crews as the slightly longer crossing time to Belfast necessitated very focused and carefully planned loading and discharging in order to maintain the schedule. Things were further complicated by construction work associated with the new HSS berths in both Belfast and Stranraer which was taking place immediately adjacent to the ramps used by the conventional ships. Looking back, it is quite remarkable that we achieved such reliability and much credit must also go to the engineers on all the ships who were quite limited in the time available for even routine maintenance.

With the arrival of the HSS *Stena Voyager*, the *Stena Antrim* was withdrawn from the route and the 'Caledonia' and the 'Galloway' were reduced to a supporting role mainly carrying freight. Next to go was the 'Galloway'. Sold to Moroccan interests she departed during February 2002, eventually to begin a new career in the Mediterranean where the former *Stena Antrim* and *Stena Cambria* were already in service.

The *Stena Caledonia* continued to serve the route subservient to the HSS but in times of bad weather would assume a higher profile when the fast craft was obliged to cancel her sailings.

Just occasionally there was bit of variety injected into the routine, such as annual refit. This was most frequently at Belfast but over the years Glasgow, Bremerhaven, Swansea and Birkenhead also featured. Always hard work and not usually blessed with good weather, they did nonetheless allow for a few good nights out and a bit of socialising.

Perhaps the most unexpected change to the routine came during the

Isle of Man TT season in 2007 and again in 2008. In a surprise move the ship was chartered by the Isle of Man Steam Packet Co. to operate weekend sailings between Douglas and Heysham. Both ports were quite a challenge in their own way, but the Steam Packet Company, then under the guidance of our former boss, Captain Hamish Ross, could not have been more helpful and we were extremely indebted to him for his willing and unstinting assistance.

To the great satisfaction of those serving on board, *Stena Caledonia* has in more recent times returned to prominence and after a major refit is again back in business carrying large numbers of passengers and freight.

Time is, however, catching up and for all connected with *St David/Stena Caledonia* over the years, seeing her go will be quite a wrench but I am sure that most will fondly remember the ship and carry happy memories with them long into the future.

It is right that we remember such a noteworthy ship, but perhaps we should also reflect on the quiet genius of Don Ripley and Tony Rogan, Sealink's Naval Architects, who conjured up solutions to the often conflicting terms of their remit to produce a design of such enduring suitability and versatility that all four 'Saint' vessels are still in service. Nor should we forget the proud shipbuilding tradition of Harland & Wolff who built these ships and to whom they were often sent for refit in succeeding years.

Finally, a ship can only be as good as its crew and I happily pay tribute to all those who over the years in all departments and ranks contributed to the success of *St David/Stena Caledonia* through their hard work and attention to detail.

Hail 'Caledonia' – a fine British ship!

The *Stena Caledonia* in Loch Ryan. (Kenneth Whyte)

Heysham

MEMORIES OF SEALINK ISLE OF MAN

Captain Ken Crellin

My memories of Sealink are almost all pleasant and positive, although I have to admit straight away that my first contact with the company came as something of a relief, as Manx Line, the company for which I then worked was in financial difficulties and sorely in need of rescue.

As it turned out Sealink had been closely watching the situation and recognised a business opportunity when they saw it. The exact details are still not public knowledge but one can imagine that owning the port of Heysham, from which Manx Line traded to the Isle of Man, Sealink were able to accurately assess the level of business and future trends and decided that for a number of reasons, the Heysham-Douglas route was a worthwhile investment.

Captain Ken Crellin. (Justin Merrigan)

Their entry was achieved, as was often the case in those days, through the good offices of James Fisher of Barrow, a private company who were able to move much more quickly than the publicly owned and legally handicapped Sealink (haste was required, as other companies were also interested in the route).

Our ship then was the *Manx Viking*, a modestly sized ro-ro vessel, formerly the *Monte Castillo* of Aznar line. She was fairly new, having run for only one season in the Mediterranean and a few trips from the Canaries to Liverpool with refrigerated fruit – a rather unusual dual role for which she was equipped with a fully insulated and refrigerated vehicle deck. The DTI were naturally unnerved at what they saw as a vehicle deck lined with apparently inflammable material and demanded that it be removed. This added great time and cost to the conversion work, contributing eventually to the

The *Manx Viking* arriving at Douglas Isle of Man in July 1979.
(Don Smith/Pictureships)

company's demise – although their caution was soon vindicated when some of the insulation did indeed catch fire during the removal process.

After their acquisition of the company, the *Manx Viking* was initially managed by Fishers, whose efficient 'deep-sea' style was sometimes a pleasant surprise for ferrymen such as ourselves. Our daily arrivals in Heysham were usually accompanied by a visit from a proper agent, who took tea with us, politely inquired as to our needs and soon became a valued and supportive friend.

Eventually, of course, the planned Sealink takeover happened, with the acquisition of a 60 per cent shareholding in the company, with Fishers retaining 40 per cent. A new Sealink manager, Martin Miller, appeared on the scene, the *Manx Viking* was thoroughly overhauled, and things began to look up.

Martin was young, dynamic and surprisingly popular, given the usual (and occasionally justified) distain with which ships' crews often regard their management. This may have been because the whole age profile of Manx

Line staff was exceptionally young – remarkably so by modern British standards. This could be partially explained by the circumstances of the company's birth – it was undoubtedly a risky venture from the beginning, and the older established officers and shore staff in other companies could not be expected to risk their livelihoods by transferring to a new service.

After our earlier tribulations, Sealink was seen as a steadying hand, and an 'onward and upward' culture was detectable with serious problems being tackled with serious money and expertise. The rest of the commercial story, including the eventual merger of Manx Line with the Isle of Man Steam Packet has been well recorded elsewhere but it is probably worth mentioning that the current success of the route goes a long way to explaining Sealink's original interest.

This piece is, however, intended as a personal reminiscence, and many tales of that period come to mind – some curious, some worrying and some amusing. One of the more pleasant duties which fell to Manx Line Masters

The *Manx Viking*. (John Hendy collection)

was to be appointed to various charter vessels as either pilot or company representative. In this role, we were privileged to meet a great variety of Sealink and other personnel, ashore and afloat.

There were many undoubted 'characters' – few more so than Captain Bill Shields of the *Antrim Princess*, chartered for one particularly stormy winter. Bill delighted in inviting a random collection of passengers to the bridge almost every trip and had a great repertoire of entertainment. One of his favourite tricks was to join the group of bridge visitors before leaving port, dressed in civvies, and pretend to be one of them. When the Captain then 'failed to turn up' he would announce that he 'had read a book on how to do it' and volunteer to take the ship to sea – which he would then do, faultlessly, of course, but to the great horror of the hapless audience.

He would also sometimes have the Chief Cook, complete with chef's hat, standing on the bridge wing, pretending to manoeuvre the ship while Bill himself actually did so, hiding inside the wheelhouse.

Questions from passengers about the difficulties of navigation across

The *Antrim Princess* arrives at Douglas. (Stan Basnett)

The *Viking Victory*. (Miles Cowsill)

the North Channel were usually met with grave admissions of previous 'failures,' this performance being ably supported by his 'straight man' – the Second Officer – who would proudly produce a wad of US dollars from his wallet, for use on those foggy occasions when the ship missed Northern Ireland altogether.

To us, of course, these japes were hilarious and helped to take some of the stress out of the appalling weather during that winter but I understand that subsequently Bill was 'persuaded' to desist by an increasingly worried Manager – perhaps not surprisingly! If you're reading this, Bill, you can rest assured we have happy memories of that time and wish you well.

A couple of the most interesting vessels chartered in by Sealink Isle of Man in those times came from Townsend Thoresen (everyone seemed to have spare ships then – how times have changed!). The *Viking III* and the *Viking Victory* were two of a class of splendid little Scandinavian ferries, tough and manoeuvrable, manned and very efficiently run by the Norwegians.

The *Earl Godwin*.
(Don Smith/Pictureships)

Interestingly, we found their personalities to be very 'Manx' in character, possibly stemming from centuries-old Viking connections. Initially dour and uncommunicative, they would carefully assess us for about a week, after which they would open up to become tremendously helpful and friendly.

They also had (to our downtrodden eyes, anyway) an incredible level of administrative freedom. At the conclusion of one charter, the Norwegian Master invited my entire family, and that of our Manager, Captain Andrew Douglas, to return with him to Le Havre, complete with our cars. On arrival, he placed the ship on the linkspan for our convenience (I believe our two modest vehicles are still the only ones to have been transported directly by ro-ro from the Isle of Man to France), and looked after us on board for several days before arranging a (free!) passage back via Southampton. Happy days!

Another vessel of the same class was Sealink's *Earl Godwin*, from the

Channel Islands, which visited us for a few weeks while the *Manx Viking* underwent her annual dry dock. That too, was an enjoyable experience, and we found the 'southerners' to be a splendidly civilised bunch. In spite of the limited 'down-time' available, they were soon energetically arranging on-board parties for the attractive young ladies in the Manx Line office – to which we were all invited, naturally.

Sadly, commercial pressure across the shipping world has now ensured that such social opportunities are rare, and more's the pity, as they often acted as a lubricant for cross-fertilisation of ideas (come on, catch up, I'm not talking about the office girls now, we're back in the grim marine world).

This was never more evident than when the Officers of the *Manx Viking*, along with local Harbourmasters, struck up a close friendship with the local RN fishery protection vessel, HMS *Lindisfarne*. Both groups were equally fascinated with each other's culture and it soon became evident that if exchanges could somehow be arranged, the RN could provide matchless training, while we in return could offer the practical, hands-on seagoing, pilotage and ship-handling experience which they felt their junior officers lacked – not to mention cabins which, to them, were comparable in size with the Royal Apartments at Windsor.

In spite of some exploratory moves, and the willingness of the Captain, David Wilson, to take some of us with him on fishery patrol (a fascinating experience) the 'exchange' ideas proved to be wishful thinking, and to this day I understand there is little opportunity for officers of either service to learn from the other. A great shame.

The Navy's covert admiration of our supposed ship-handling skills was sometimes evident on arrival in Douglas, when during berthing of the *Manx Viking*, a large proportion of the naval crew would suddenly pop up from behind the bulwarks of the *Lindisfarne*, holding large scorecards, which frequently averaged nine or more – flattering, but probably undeserved, considering our bow thrust was a luxury unknown to them!

In the matter of laconic maritime humour, our continental cousins were not far behind. When the old, but quite adequate, French ferry *Villandry* was pressed into service one summer, SNCF were unable to provide more than a couple of their own officers, and we found ourselves suddenly the sole incumbents of a foreign vessel, having to dig deeply into our school French to find out how to make her go forwards and backwards. Fortunately this was before the days of Safety Management Systems and Induction procedures and somehow we managed.

A few weeks later, we returned her to Calais in beautiful summer weather and were greeted by a couple of cheerful SNCF officers who presented us with our tickets back to England. They suggested that we quickly sign the handover document and hurry as the bus was waiting to take us to the terminal. I had to explain that there may have to be a delay, as I had just been informed that an electrical fire had broken out in one of the switchboards and we were considering at that moment whether to sound the emergency alarm. I had assumed that the 'owners representatives' would be at least slightly reluctant to take delivery of their vessel in such an incendiary condition but they were quite unfazed; "…don't worry, Capitaine…it happens often… allez vite…sign here – the bus is waiting…."

I can only guess that as human life was not at stake and they could assume that the insurance settlement would probably exceed the actual value of the the vessel, the situation was not of great concern. In the event, our

The French *Villandry* leaving Douglas for Heysham. (Stan Basnett)

heroic electrician joined the bus after us, having apparently beaten out the flames with his suitcase, leaving the *Villandry* to sail another day – which indeed she did for many years under Greek ownership.

Coincidentally, fire also played a part in another, slightly embarrassing episode aboard the *Antrim Princess* (which was then 'our ship', having been sub-chartered to the newly merged Manx Line/Isle of Man Steam Packet and renamed *Tynwald*), fortunately again without serious consequences.

We were asked by a quite respectable religious organisation to transport a symbolic lamp, which had been lit on the shores of Galilee and then taken around the world to spread the Word. As the 'constant flame' had already been carried through the deserts of Arabia, the frozen wastes of Afghanistan and even, to our astonishment, on a Boeing 747, this was a responsibility which we took seriously – anxious as always to please our customers.

The problem, however, was that the International Dangerous Goods Code was rather vague on the carriage of naked flames on ro-ro vehicle decks. Eventually, the Radio Officer (we carried such well-educated chaps in those days) observed that as he was permitted to smoke in the Radio Room, the lamp could be classed as a 'cigarette' of sorts, and he would look after it. For added safety, we suggested placing it in a galvanised bucket, thus demonstrating our slender grasp of physics when it was deprived of oxygen and promptly went out.

Obviously Satan was at work in the confines of the Radio Room (something we had long suspected), and as the project was believed to be supported by a Director of the Company and several senior members of the Isle of Man Legislature, we concluded that the cause of Christianity (and our own careers) would be best served by keeping our mouths shut and re-lighting the lamp on arrival.

Only now, at a safe distance of 30 years, can the truth be told!

Before leaving the subject of Sealink, it would be remiss to omit mention of the support of the Head Office staff at Eversholt House. From the first day, those aboard the *Manx Viking* felt we were accepted as 'family' and much appreciated the levels of professionalism we found throughout the company.

All staff were strongly encouraged, by means of generous travel concessions to 'use the system' – i.e. to travel by train and ship, report any problems, and pass on their acquired knowledge and hopefully enthusiasm, to family friends and acquaintances, thus acting as an effective additional marketing tool.

Perhaps in these parsimonious days, marine accountants would tell us that costs were unsustainably high, etc., but looking back at the apparent

▲ The *Duke of Argyll* alongside at Heysham in July 1969. Along with her sisters, the *Duke of Lancaster* and the *Duke Rothesay,* the 'Argyll' was the mainstay of British Rail's services to and from Belfast since 1956. Although these classic ships were converted to stern loading car ferries in 1970, the decline in traffic, exacerbated by political unrest in Northern Ireland, brought the closure of the historic passenger link in 1975. It was not until the arrival of the *Manx Viking* that Heysham became a passenger port once again. (Don Smith/Pictureships)

smooth efficiency of the British Rail/Sealink interface, I suspect that at a national level, something valuable has been lost (or so it seems to me – don't forget, we Manxies are easily impressed by fast trains – ours here on the Isle of Man are still driven by steam to this day, seldom exceeding 30 mph… and are rarely late or cancelled incidentally, but that's another story).

SHIP HANDLING

No history of the *Manx Viking* and her various running mates would be complete without mention of the interesting handling characteristics of the various vessels – a matter of vital importance to all ferry Masters, but rarely discussed elsewhere.

This may be because the hydrodynamics are even now not fully understood and vary greatly from ship to ship. An airline pilot can be fairly confident that the 737 he is flying today will respond to the controls in exactly the same way as the one he flew yesterday. This does not apply, unfortunately, to ships. Identical vessels from one shipyard may feel broadly the same but large groups of 'sisters' are unusual in the maritime world and as a Master moves from one vessel to another, he will encounter a wide range of characteristics – some predictable, some not.

A notable exception to this rule, incidentally, is the series of 74-metre fast ferries built by Incat of Tasmania, but even they have their own idiosyncrasies that the Masters must be wary of.

Perhaps one should start at the beginning with a broad outline of the way in which vessels are controlled and manoeuvred. In single screw ships, the rudder is placed directly in the wash from the propeller and even at slow speed will provide a sideways force when required. A great disadvantage of the single screw arrangement is that a forward thrust is applied at the same time, moving the ship ahead.

To improve matters, ships were soon designed with two engines and two propellers, side by side, so that if one was running ahead, the other could be operated astern and so keep the vessel stationary. (There were other reasons too for multi-engine layouts – for a given power, less vertical space was required in the engine room and propellers could be smaller, reducing draught).

Unfortunately, for many years, designers continued to place a single rudder in the middle, out of the wash from both propellers and fairly useless when manoeuvring at slow speeds. This was alleviated to some extent by the 'transverse thrust' effect when operating the propellers in opposite directions.

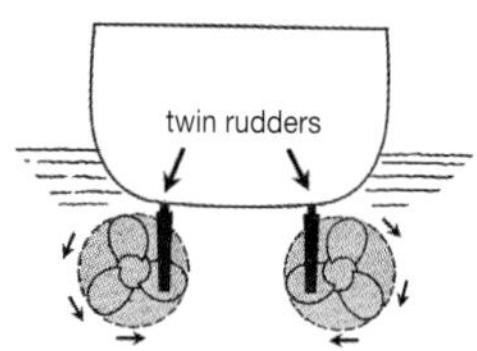

Both engines going ahead

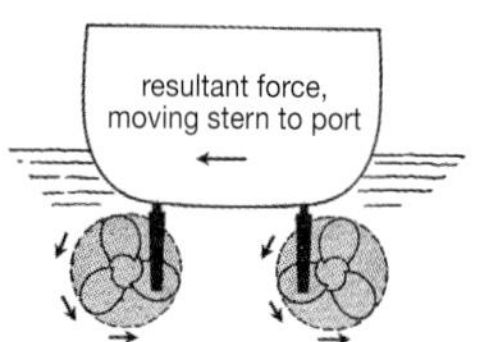

Port engine ahead, stbd engine astern – both screws now rotating anti-clockwise

For those not familiar with this effect, the illustration on the left may help.

Early ferries, particularly the generation of turbine vessels built in the first half of the twentieth century, were usually fitted with 'fixed-pitch' propellers, the rotation of which had to be reversed when going astern, thus satisfactorily producing the above effects.

Modern vessels now have 'variable-pitch' propellers, where only the pitch angle of the blades is reversed when going astern and the screws themselves continue to turn in their original directions (one clockwise, one anticlockwise). Clearly therefore, the 'wheeling effects' are permanently opposed and there is no transverse thrust force – the only sideways force being provided by the comparatively weak push-pull effect of the shafts. Because of this weakness, modern variable-pitch ferries are usually now fitted with twin rudders, so that at least one rudder (the one behind the ahead-going screw) will provide a satisfactory sideways force.

Unfortunately, the introduction of variable-pitch propellers preceded the realisation that they really required twin rudders and a whole generation of variable-pitch vessels were built with a single rudder, making them very difficult to manoeuvre.

The *Manx Viking* in fact was one of these and Masters soon learned that although the bow of the vessel could be positioned quite well using the bow thrust unit, the stern certainly could not. It was therefore usually preferable to approach the berth stern first, steering the vessel with the bow thrusters, secure a stern line to hold the stern in place, and then bring the bow alongside later. Hardly a neat or convenient procedure when compared with modern twin-rudder practice where both ends of the vessel can usually be moved smoothly sideways together. Single-rudder vessels like the *Manx Viking* sometimes required several attempts at berthing in strong winds – but as in all things, we simply got used to it (although not without expressing our robust opinions of ship designers on a daily basis!).

It will be appreciated that if berthing bow-on to a linkspan, the vessel had to be brought ahead of the berth and then backed towards it in order to carry out the above manoeuvre and in some berths, notably Douglas, there is no room to do this. As luck would have it, however, it was quickly realised that 'bow-loading' was not an advantage with the types of freight trailer carried and stern-to berthing became the norm in both ports served.

The story of the *Manx Viking* was not all bad, however. With comparatively deep draught for a vessel of her size, she was regarded as a very comfortable vessel at sea. I well remember our very first southerly gale when leaving Douglas. We were all used to the narrow, sharp bows of the earlier Steam

Packet vessels and on rounding Douglas Head, we braced ourselves for the inevitable 'plunge' into the first big swell. To our surprise, the *Manx Viking* simply lowered her nose gently into it, cushioned by the bulbous bow, and made her way to Heysham slowly and gently (she was no greyhound) hardly disturbing the watchkeepers' coffee mugs on the forward console.

Her fairly modest righting lever (a measure of the force tending to 'right' a vessel when heeled) assisted this gentle behaviour at sea in most weather, but following seas were rather less fun, with her wide stern and sometimes worrying tendency to pause at the extremity of a deep roll.

Manoeuvrability though, was certainly not her strong point, and it was always interesting to experience more capable vessels. Notable among these

The *Manx Viking* at Heysham. (Captain Ken Crellin)

were the *Viking III* and the *Viking Victory*. Tough little ferries with twin rudders and widely separated shafts, obviously designed for tight spots, which could approach the harbour entrance almost at right angles if required, and thrown around, virtually on the spot, with complete confidence. Being short, they pitched rather heavily in a head sea but were nevertheless popular with Masters and passengers alike.

Rather more sedate, but still a pleasure to handle were Sealink's *Ailsa Princess* and SNCF's *Villandry* – both twin rudder vessels, although we were to become much more familiar with the 'Ailsa's' older sister, the *Antrim Princess*, which became the *Tynwald*, on the Heysham route. Although a

The *Ailsa Princess* moves astern to the linkspan at Douglas. (Stan Basnett)

fine vessel in her day, the *Tynwald* was showing her age a little by then and was fitted with a rather weak bow thruster – also a common feature of early ships. Nevertheless, her handling was decidedly superior to the *Manx Viking*, although she was nowhere near as comfortable at sea.

Before leaving the subject of handling characteristics, mention should be made of two more features of great concern to the Master, the first being stopping power – the brakes!

Approaching port at very slow speed can be fraught with danger as wind and tide have a comparatively greater effect on the vessel and can cause serious deflections from a chosen line of approach. Masters therefore generally find it safer to approach at a respectable speed, which makes stopping power an important consideration. Sadly, modern ferries tend to

The *Villandry* swinging at Douglas. (Stan Basnett)

be rather deficient in this department, for a number of reasons – not all of them known to me. Contributory factors probably include propellers designed exclusively with ahead-going fuel economy in mind, rather than astern power (low fuel consumption sells ships, manoeuvrability unfortunately doesn't) and a tendency towards 'constant speed' engines in which the propeller always revolves at full speed, control being achieved through pitch variation alone – producing lots of bubbles and cavitation when going astern.

To add to the problem, both Douglas and Heysham were constructed over a century ago, with much smaller ships in mind, so stopping and manoeuvring space inside is very restricted.

Finally there is the consideration of what Masters call 'windage' – the pressure of wind on the side of the vessel, causing her to drift, either bodily or at one end, causing her to rotate. This is the enemy, of course – the major reason why ships need to be fitted with the sophisticated equipment we have talked about. Comparatively deep-draughted ships like the *Manx Viking* are less prone to this problem, having more 'grip' on the water, and indeed that ship was fairly well 'balanced' – drifting downwind more or less bodily with little rotation.

In comparison, many recent ferries – like the Isle of Man Steam Packet's *Ben-my-Chree* for example – have a large block of accommodation well forward, acting like a sail to propel the fore end of the ship downwind, while the stern remains in place or even in extreme cases rotates upwind – such tendencies often need to be corrected by fitting a more powerful thrusters unit than might otherwise be required.

If all the foregoing sounds like a salty wringing of hands, perhaps it is – ferry Masters are not noted for their reticence when describing the shortcomings of their various vessels. It also has to be said that over the years a remarkable number of ships have been placed into service (at considerable expense) in ports for which they are patently unsuited.

Although it has to be said that even Sealink in the later years were guilty of a few 'lemons' here and there (remember they purchased the *Lune Bridge* and the *Lagan Bridge*? – single rudders again – and no bridge wing controls!) but in general they stood out as highly respected designers of the right ship in the right place. The *Hengist* class on the south coast were memorable and I was fortunate enough to command one of the similar ships to that group in her later years, the *King Orry* – formerly the *Saint Eloi*. They were splendid ships – comfortable at sea, predictable in port, reliable and liked by Masters, crews and passengers.

Holyhead

MY TIME WITH IRISH CROSS CHANNEL SERVICES

Captain Trevor Salmon

Having obtained my Master's Foreign Going Certificate after ten years with Shaw Savill and Albion and their associated company, the Aberdeen and Commonwealth Line, I joined British Rail Shipping Services operating from the port of Holyhead in December 1961. My first ship was the coal burning cattle and general cargo vessel *Slieve More*. A total of 32 years and 24 ships later, I retired having made 3,398 round trip crossings on the Irish Sea.

During that time I had many experiences, some enjoyable, some not so enjoyable and some very satisfying. From the time of the coal burning ships many changes took place in Holyhead which made life both more challenging and provided better working conditions. The introduction of the *Slieve Donard* enabled livestock to be carried in better conditions. Then the drive-on, drive-off *Holyhead Ferry I*, on which I made the inaugural trip in July 1965 into the temporary terminal at Dun Laoghaire, enabled cars to be driven on board rather than being craned on, as took place on the Mail Ships *Cambria* and *Hibernia*.

Captain Trevor Salmon berths the *Stena Hibernia* at Dun Laoghaire in 1991. (Justin Merrigan)

On the cargo side of Holyhead's operations, 1965 also saw the introduction of the *Harrogate* which carried containers, leading to the introduction in 1970 of the cellular container ships *Brian Boroime* and *Rhodri Mawr*, on all of which I sailed, latterly as Master. In those years nearly all the crews came from Holyhead or lived on Anglesey and they were all very happy ships on which to sail.

I recall two difficult times I experienced when sailing as Master. The first was the engine room fire on the *Brian Boroime* off the Isle of Man when on passage to Belfast. This fire disabled one engine and the bridge steering. There were no casualties and the ship was able to return to Holyhead on one engine. The second incident was also a fire, this time on the *St David* in Dun Laoghaire in April 1988 when the Chief Engineer was missing until rescued by the local fire brigade. Both fires were caused by fractured fuel lines.

In later years, I was fortunate enough to be asked to make some interesting trips on behalf of the Company and I also relieved the Marine Superintendent and Harbour Master when necessary. One trip was to Colombo with the Marine Superintendent to assess the suitability of the *Tackler Dosinia* to operate in Holyhead. I was also Master for the trials of the *Seafreight Highway* off Piraeus and brought the *Seafreight Freeway* from Landskrona in Sweden to moorings in the River Blackwater.

The *Holyhead Ferry 1* at Holyhead's Salt Island terminal. (David Jones)

The *Seafreight Highway* was quite an experience, not really having been abroad by myself for a while and having to cope with all the requirements of a foreign port's paperwork. I had to attend a briefing at Eversholt House as there were complications with the unions because the ship was registered in Bermuda. Once things had been sorted out I flew from Heathrow to Athens staying overnight at a hotel in Piraeus. The next morning I joined the ship which was berthed in Perama. The next day we did sea trials south of Piraeus with Compass adjusting, D>F> calibration, bow thrust tests then steaming runs off Hydra. We anchored for the night 3.5 miles south of Piraeus then next morning proceeded to a lay-up berth at Kinosoura. The following day the shut down was completed and I returned home for a couple of days before flying out to Landskrona in Sweden to join the *Seafreight Freeway* which was having new ramp wires and a passenger certificate survey. After a couple of days we sailed for the River Blackwater where the ship was laid up on a swivel mooring.

However, the ship which was closest to my heart was the *St Columba*,

The *Rhodri Mawr* and *Brian Boroime* at Holyhead. (Chris Howell)

The *Seafreight Highway* in Greece. (Captain Glynne Pritchard)

later the *Stena Hibernia,* from which I retired as Senior Master. I was on the delivery trip from Aalborg in 1977 and later oversaw the conversion of the ship in Bremerhaven by Stena Line.

The thing I remember most on the *St Columba*'s delivery from Aalborg is the decision that had to be made by Captain Evans whether with a new ship and crew he went north about through the Pentland Firth, the most direct route, or through the English Channel and round Land's End. The weather forecast when we sailed was for strong winds around the north of Scotland and the decision was made to go south about although it meant we had to call in at Dover to refuel. I am sure it was the wisest decision, for even with the weather we had and being light ship we had quite a 'bumpy' ride. Fortunately, we carried the charts required for either route but I remember as Second Officer it gave me quite a lot of extra work having to chart the courses for both routes before a final decision was made. The decision also gave the chance to see how the ship reacted in varying weather conditions and gave a daytime arrival in Holyhead for the welcoming crowds.

Being Senior Master for the refit and conversion of the passenger and crew accommodation on the *St Columba* in Bremerhaven was a very interesting experience. We arrived in Bremerhaven on 11th January 1991 and I stayed with the ship the whole time until we got back to Holyhead on 11th March. Those with me had a break during that period but my wife Mary came out and stayed with me for a fortnight which made a nice break. The whole of the passenger and crew accommodation was gutted and refitted to Stena requirements and it really made her into a different, more open plan ship. She had given 14 years of good service but during that period time had moved on and the refit of the accommodation enabled her to meet adequately the requirements of a more modern age as the *Stena Hibernia*.

I feel so fortunate to have sailed with so many fine officers and crew and to have had the opportunity of sailing on the various ships which operated from Holyhead between 1961 and 1993.

WILD VENTURE!

Captain George Davey

In August 1964 the *Slieve More* was involved in the salvage of the yacht *Wild Venture*, which had been stolen from the Menai Straits. The theft followed the escape of one of the Great Train Robbers from prison and there was speculation that the yacht was being used in the getaway.

The *Slieve More* at Dublin. (John Hendy collection)

The naval destroyer sent to capture the yacht broke down. The *Slieve More* was on passage from Dublin when we spotted the yacht and preparations were made to come alongside her. She was motoring west with no crew apparent. Our Chief Engineer was Jack Sharp and as he had yachting experience was nominated to take charge of the boarding party, which was formed from the many volunteers in the crew.

As the *Slieve More* went alongside the yacht, the lookout alerted me to the submarine that had surfaced astern! It had apparently been monitoring the situation from periscope depth, but had been unable to board the moving yacht because of the submarine's hull shape. With careful manoeuvring our boarding party was able to jump aboard the yacht from the cattle doors in the side of the ship. Rather than heavily armed bank robbers, they found two sleeping teenagers below deck!

The *Wild Venture* sailed back to Holyhead under Jack Sharp's command, and the two young men were handed over to the police. The incident caused some amusement in the national press. The crew of the *Slieve More* eventually received a small amount in salvage from the insurers of the yacht.

Captain Len Evans. (photo courtesy Eleanor Evans)

CAPTAIN LEN EVANS AND THE *ST COLUMBA*

Justin Merrigan

In April 1948 a young Len Evans joined British Railways at Holyhead. Following service as a deck officer on the cargo and mail boats, Captain Evans's first commands were on the four 'Slieve' cargo vessels operating between Holyhead and Dublin. His first passenger command came in 1966 when he became Master of the *Hibernia*. It was not long before he found himself in the new car ferry *Holyhead Ferry I* and also the *Dover*.

In 1976 Captain Evans was appointed Senior Master of the new car ferry then under construction and in April 1977 he commanded the *St Columba* on her delivery trip from Denmark to the Irish Sea. This was a time of celebration for all connected with the link and on Wednesday 27th April the new ship undertook her inaugural voyage to Dun Laoghaire with members of the Irish Government, British Rail Board, tour operators, journalists and other VIPs on board. There were two sets of officers on board; Captain Evans, and Captain John Peters as Masters, the latter taking her out of Holyhead. Walter Lloyd Williams and Lewis Pritchard as Mates. Trevor Salmon and Dai Davies as 2nd Mates and Tudor Jones and Glynne Pritchard as 3rd Mates. That evening, guests attended a Dinner

The *Duke of Lancaster* and *St Columba* off Holyhead. (Chris Howell)

▲ Under the command of Captain Len Evans, the *Duke of Rothesay* hauls herself off the berth at Salt Island in 1975. Speaking of the Heysham Dukes, Captain Evans recalled, “They were well built ships, and fast too, but lacked the manoeuvrability that all cross channel ships should have. Their bow rudders were more effective than their main rudder. The *Duke of Rothesay*, which I had for some time, had a turning circle of 5 and a half cables, while the *St Columba* could, if one tried, do it in three quarters of a cable.” (John Hendy collection)

at the Royal Marine Hotel, addressed by An Taoiseach (Irish Premier) Mr Liam Cosgrave TD. The Chairman of British Rail, Mr Peter Parker offered a toast to the new ship: "The *St Columba* as a symbol of strengthened ties between the people of Ireland, the people of Britain and the people of Europe."

When he retired in September 1986 Captain Evans had served over 48 years at sea, 25 of which were in command – making him the most senior Master in the Sealink fleet.

Captain Evans was also a loyal union member, joining the NEOU in 1942 and transferring to the MMSA in 1962. He joined the Mercantile Marine Service Association Council in 1977 and held the posts of deputy vice-president and vice-president before becoming MMSA president in 1985. Through his involvement in the MMSA, Captain Evans became increasingly dedicated to the welfare of seafarers – being closely involved with the care of retired seafarers and their dependants at the Mariners' Park complex in Wallasey and the Union's charitable functions, chairing the Welfare Funds Committee from 1985 to 1999.

In 1993, to mark 16 years of service on the MMSA working to expand and improve the warfare facilities for elderly retired seafarers and their partners at the 16-acre Mariners Park complex in Wallasey, Captain Evans was presented with the Nevins and Griffiths Award by the Merchant Navy officers' union NUMAST. Former colleagues at Holyhead recommended to NUMAST Council that Captain Evans be considered for the award, a move forwarded by Captain Tudor Jones on behalf of active members and seconded by Captain Glynne Pritchard on behalf of retired members. It was typical of the admiration and respect still held at the port for their former Senior Master seven years after his retirement.

Captain Evans crossed the bar on 20th July 2005. In tribute to his work with the officer's union, now known as NAUTILUS, a special memorial garden was opened at Mariners' Park retirement complex in September 2006.

PRAYER ON THE *DOVER*

Captain Len Evans

During September 1974 we left Holyhead with the *Dover* in flat calm conditions but it was a good Force 12 Northerly in Dun Laoghaire. I was able to berth, although the sea in the harbour was such that she was pitching and rolling alongside the berth.

Clearly she was going to suffer major damage and so I sailed back out into Dublin Bay where I turned circles for the next 12 hours until conditions improved slightly and I was able to go back alongside, discharge cars and passengers and reload.

At about 23.00 I had a message from the RAF at Valley that the wind was now 83 mph. Coming into Holyhead was not funny and at one stage it seemed inevitable that she would smash into the Refit Berth. However, she came around and I was delighted to dock in the Station Berth.

After we got alongside, the Carpenter came up to my cabin, which he never usually did and with tears rolling down his cheeks said, "Captain, I prayed for you and she came around."

He left me a very chastened man!

The *Dover* comes astern onto the Admiralty Pier at Holyhead. (Justin Merrigan Collection)

THE *ST COLUMBA*

Captain Len Evans

Thursday 15th July 1976 saw a chartered Aer Lingus 737 fly from Dublin, via Heathrow, with a representative group of British and Irish guests to witness the launch of the new *St Columba*. The following day saw high winds, the direction of which caused the level of water in Lim Fjord, on which Aalborg stands, to drop. With the water level just four inches too low to safely take the new ship, the invited guests had to settle for the naming ceremony which went ahead with Mrs Joan Kirby, wife of British Rail's Shipping and International Services Division's general manager David Kirby, performing the honours. With suitable tidal conditions the *St Columba* finally took to the water on Friday 16th July with Mrs Kirby launching the vessel, unfortunately after the departure of the guests for London and Dublin on their pre-arranged charter flight.

Sea trials were carried out in the Kattegat over the weekend of 18th March 1977 and at 05.00 on Saturday 2nd April the *St Columba* sailed from Aalborg for Holyhead. On the following day the ship arrived at Dover's Western Docks where minor engine adjustments were carried out. The next morning the *St Columba* was on her way again and at 14.00 on Tuesday 5th April she arrived at her new home port to be given a rapturous welcome by more than 5,000 people crowding every vantage point to see the new ship. Although the weather conditions on the delivery voyage did not exceed Force 7, the ship behaved admirably, and her sea-keeping qualities lived up to our best expectations. This was of course further confirmed after she went into service and in the subsequent winter.

Saturday 19th December 1981 saw the Irish Sea at its worst, this being the night the Penlee Lifeboat RNLB *Solomon Browne* was lost with her entire crew going to the aid of the coaster *Union Star* in the western English Channel.

On the *St Columba* we had a long first passage in our 24 hours on. With winds at Force 12+ the ship was hove to off the Kish Tower for eight hours, conditions at Dun Laoghaire being impossible to even consider an attempt at berthing. We eventually got alongside at Dun Laoghaire at 06.30 the following morning, 14 hours after leaving Holyhead.

In December 1982, unable to berth at Dun Laoghaire due to a south-east gale Force 11-12, I steamed slowly south from the Kish lighthouse. In the vicinity of the Codling I found myself looking up at the sea from the bridge! Needless to say I did not stay down there for long and was most surprised when a German ship called me up asking if I could assist him because he, as the giving way vessel, was concerned not to alter course because his cargo of phosphates could ship. One touch on the *St Columba*'s telegraphs and she was away like a scalded cat, much to the admiration and relief of the German.

MAIL BOAT MOVEMENTS

Captain John Bakewell

I joined the Holyhead ships on 14th April 1958. It was a beautiful evening when I stepped aboard the *Slieve Bloom* to be met by the Officer of the Watch – the late Alun Thomas. The first thing he said to me was, "This is a soul destroying job!" Needless to say I stayed for 33 years!

The regular pattern for the Holyhead mail boats *Hibernia* and *Cambria* was for one nightly sailing in each direction on a year-round basis. This was increased to a second sailing in each direction during the summer months with a third at peak periods taken by the *Princess Maud*.

A mail boat would leave Holyhead at 03.15 at the start of a 48-hour cycle. On the Irish side, she would lie over all day prior to taking the evening sailing at 20.45. It became a local pastime to walk the pier to watch the mail boat sail or shift around the Carlisle Pier from the arrival to the departure berth.

These manoeuvres were always of interest to the locals and at times it seemed as if the whole town assembled to watch the proceedings. At the seaward end of the Carlisle Pier there was a large bollard. On the quay was a junk (a very large coir rope) with a thick steel wire attached to it. At the end of the coir rope there was a very large eye splice for dropping over the bitts on the ship aft. In the eye splice there was a smaller rope (a messenger). The wire part was for putting around the bollard ashore. You ended up with a few turns of wire rope around the shore bollard, then the coir rope with its eye splice over the ship's bitts.

When ready to shift ship, we singled up to a headline and a stern line with

Captain John Bakewell

The *Hibernia* leaving Holyhead.
(Don Smith/Pictureships)

The *Cambria* warping around the pier at Dun Laoghaire. (John Byrne)

the engines all ready. The Chief Officer usually did this manoeuvre. Then, "Let go fore and aft and slow astern on the starboard engine." As she went astern, the after crowd threw a heaving line ashore which was quickly made fast to the messenger. It was then quickly taken to the winch and hauled aboard until the eye of the junk could be put over the bitts. Steadily the weight would come on the junk and the ship would start to swing round the quay with the starboard engine still on slow astern. When nearly round, the Chief Officer would stop the engine and order "Let go". The shore gang would slack off on the wire and the men aft would heave on the eye until it could be thrown off. When clear, the engines would be put astern and the ship would glide into its berth on the east side. A large axe was always to hand in case the rope should jam on the bitts. In seamanship manuals, you would find that putting an eye over the bitts would be frowned upon! However, this procedure worked in Dun Laoghaire for a great number of years.

At Holyhead shifting ship was also the norm. Having arrived from Dun Laoghaire just after midnight the Chief Officer would usually shift the ship over on ropes from the mail arrival berth to the mail departure berth at about 07.30. The shore gang would wash down first and on completion of this would call the duty officer and commence the shift. These berths were at the Station Hotel end of the harbour, which was its narrowest part. The bow would be hove out to a position midway between the berths and held in position by a head rope and check ropes whilst the stern was pulled over. Two bow ropes were left out, as was the stern check rope, which was secured to a slip hook on the Arrival Berth. At sailing time the bow was first pulled out as before and held in position whilst the stern was pulled out. A member of the shore gang stood by the slip hook and on hearing a blast on the chief officer's ACME Thunderer mouth whistle would smartly strike the slip hook with a hammer to release the rope, the bow ropes being let go at the same time. The stern rope would be winched back on board as quickly as possible and the Second Officer would signal all clear on the telegraph as the eye came out of the water. During the summer when double sailings took place, the rope shift took place as soon as the departure berth was clear.

FIRE IN THE *ST COLUMBA*

Captain John Bakewell

During the morning passage from Dun Laoghaire on the last day of January 1991, I was sitting in my cabin on the *St Columba* when the phone rang. It was our Chief Engineer, John Roberts informing me that we had a fire in the Engine Room.

The *St Columba*. (Justin Merrigan)

We had to stop both engines and after some 20 minutes the fire was brought under control by the crew. Unfortunately, with so much oil around it was deemed to be unsafe to attempt to restart the port engine and so a tug from Holyhead was sent for with firemen on board.

When the tug was made fast, in appalling weather, we began the tow towards Holyhead. We were only making 1 knot for the first few hours but eventually arrived off the breakwater. A very real danger was getting caught in the ebb tide when off South Stack, so course and speed (what there was of it) had to be adjusted so that we would get the benefit of the flood tide off the Stacks.

Norman Williams, our Purser, did a fine job looking after our passengers. We had very little smoke coming into the accommodation because fans had been turned off and fire shutters were in position.

It was a great relief to berth at Salt Island around midnight. I berthed her bow in where it was still possible to discharge cars. Fortunately the bow thrust was working OK!

Captain Neville Lester and the *Lady of Mann*. Captain Lester recalls, "After several years in the container ships *Rhodri Mawr* and *Brian Boroime*, also the *St Columba*, as a deck officer and Master, I found myself in command of the Isle of Man Steam Packet's *Lady of Mann* on charter to Sealink in February 1990.

No bow and stern doors, but a side loader with manual ramps pushed into the opened shell doors for loading. The doors themselves seemed rather flimsy to me and on one occasion, a door became unseated and ended up in the dock at Holyhead's "Sheerlegs" berth, from which divers had to retrieve it!

What the "Lady" lacked in size, she certainly made up for in performance, being reasonably comfortable in a seaway and particularly manoeuvrable for berthing. I quickly became familiar with her beautiful handling capabilities and once successfully put her alongside the Sheerlegs berth in a very strong easterly (almost directly onshore wind). She worked against the wind like a dream!

At the end of the charter, I had the pleasure of taking her to Birkenhead for lay-up and return to the Steam Packet. This entailed her regular Master, Captain Vernon Kinley, joining the ship at Holyhead as my Douglas Pilot and the next day, on arrival Douglas, the Steam Packet's Commodore, Captain Eddie Fargher, joined as my Mersey Pilot. The IoM Masters were wonderful fellows and it was my pleasure to serve with them." (Justin Merrigan)

The cause was really a design fault. Our 3rd Engineer did really well in shutting down the oil flow immediately and all my crew did a great job. The only injury was to a fireman who broke his arm and the others were seasick.

SHIP HANDLING PERFECTION

Captain Neville Lester

The late Captain John Peters was an officer in the P.S.N.C. prior to joining the Holyhead ships. He was a quiet and unassuming man and was a legendary ship handler. He was also an expert in photography and had a penchant for O.P. cigarettes!

I can recall one example of his legendary ship handling. I was Duty Officer and was with Captain Cyril Powell on the bridge of the *Cambria* secure alongside the east side of the Carlisle Pier at Dun Laoghaire with a westerly gale blowing right on to the west side of the Pier; the tide was middle to high water. The *Holyhead Ferry 1* had been outside for some time with Captain Peters in command.

To my astonishment, and also that of Captain Powell, the 'Ferry 1' approached the west side at some speed. When she was almost in her berth position, but approximately 50 yards off, John dropped his starboard anchor and went full astern on his port engine and slow ahead on his starboard engine, putting the rudder hard-a-port. As the operation developed he adjusted engines and rudder to suit. She came alongside beautifully and, as we would say, wouldn't have cracked a nut!

Captain Powell looked at me and said, "John, you're a bloody hero!"

THE NIGHT OF THE 'BIG ROLL'

Captain Bill Moss

There was barely a breath of wind as the *Stena Hibernia* lay alongside in Dun Laoghaire loading for the 20.45 sailing to Holyhead. Of course, the great landmass above Dun Laoghaire sheltered the town from the SSW'ly gale that was blowing in the Irish Sea.

The Master had instructed the loading officer to 'storm load' and this involved stowing all the freight vehicles 'block-stowed', three lanes either side of the centre casing secured with our ratchet/strap lashings. The cars were loaded at both the for'd and after ends of the main vehicle deck. No mezzanine decks were in use.

We sailed 'right time' out of Dun Laoghaire, the engine room and on-board services having been advised of the weather conditions outside. Approaching the Kish Light we started to feel the wind although sea conditions were good as we were still in the lee of the Codling bank, but it wasn't too long before the passage became uncomfortable.

I know it was somewhere around that time that I decided to go up to the bridge to 'have a look at the sea' and that is indeed what I saw. I'd only been on the bridge for a few minutes when the ship dropped into a trough in the quartering sea. A large foam-capped swell appeared on the starboard quarter which seemed to tower over the ship as she lay heeling to starboard the trough. Like a 'kelly doll' she was thrown over to port to an angle that was in excess of the parameters of the bridge inclinometer (it jammed full over). With the same violence she rolled back to starboard and to a similar angle. And there we were, frozen in a moment of time, staring at our destiny in the form of another very large swell approaching like an express train. In that moment I hoped that this wall of water would not have the same effect again but of course it did. Over we went again to port and back to starboard. It felt as though we were on our beam ends. The bridge was wrecked. If it could move, it did and if it couldn't move, it soon found a way of doing so. How we managed to keep our feet I don't know! How the engines kept going I don't know! Even through all of this, the Captain and helmsman managed to steer the ship out of this synchronous rolling pattern.

And so she settled down. I was despatched to the car deck to check on the cargo. I was met at the bottom of the stairs by the car deck watchman, who was in a state of fright having lost his footing and slid under a lorry; thankfully, he was okay. My rapid assessment indicated that the lorries had shifted to port but the block stow had restricted that movement. However, some of the cars, particularly at the for'd end, were badly damaged. In fact

The *Stena Hibernia*. (Justin Merrigan)

the cars had re-stowed themselves and resembled the order of a scrapyard. They had not fared well.

Back in the passenger accommodation, there was absolute mayhem. The 'hotel' accommodation had reverted back to true; a ship. Potted plants, fixtures and fittings, decorations, cabinets, tables and chairs had all become mobile. Even the corner of a heavy gaming table had tried to gain exit through a window. And amongst all of this were the passengers who were very frightened. Many people had suffered injury but thankfully the majority were of a minor nature. The bureau staff had assumed control of the situation and took charge of the catering crew in organising First Aid, taking passenger details, and clearing areas of debris. Plates in the restaurant and bottles in the duty-free shop were in the main all broken. The engine room had fared well. All equipment had been well secured and had survived the roll.

The remainder of the voyage was far less eventful although rough. Eventually we made the lee of the North Stack and entered the calm waters of Holyhead harbour with a 3½ degrees port list. Waiting for us on the quay were

▶ Captain John Francis Sinnott pictured in his typical ship handling mode. Many shipmasters smoked whilst piloting and manoeuvring their ships in those days, a practice surely prohibited in today's Health & Safety conscious world.

John was a real character, respected by all who worked with him, ashore and afloat. His often coloured turns of phrase on anticipated impending disaster and observations on life at sea in general, voiced in his inimitable quick fire Liverpool accent, relieved many a tense moment, and belied his skill as a shipmaster par excellence.

Unconventional in so many ways, he had pet names for almost everything and anyone. The bow thrust was always the 'chuffter' and if he found himself wishing the *St Columba*'s unit had a bit more power he could be heard exclaiming that there wasn't enough 'uff in the chuff'!

At Dun Laoghaire in all weathers, but particularly during an easterly gale, he would notice the representative of the Harbour Master, or 'Harbour Munster', the Harbour 'Constabule', standing by the ramp on the berth 'just waiting for me to 't**t the piles'!

John passed away after a short retirement on 30th January 1997, but he will be long remembered with affection by all who knew him. (Justin Merrigan)

approximately 13 ambulances for the injured, the press, and a whole team of Sealink Stena staff to assist the passengers. When the passengers were called to the vehicle deck, I was amazed. There was silence; nothing was said, as though the piled up cars were a normal feature. The rest of the day was spent with the fire brigade with hydraulic equipment trying to separate the lorries. I think the worst damage to a lorry was perhaps a broken wing mirror.

THE *STENA SAILER*

Justin Merrigan

Taken on charter from Stena Line, the arrival of the *Stena Sailer* at Holyhead in 1987 marked the reintroduction of a second ship on the service to Dun Laoghaire after a gap of over two years. A far cry from the previous 'second ship', the *St David*, the *Stena Sailer* was nevertheless welcomed as a chance to build freight levels. In her initial months her continued operation was somewhat touch and go, but as traffic levels increased so her future was secured and eventually she was purchased and renamed *St Cybi*.

The ship was collected from lay-up at Falmouth and brought to Holyhead at the start of her bareboat charter to Sealink British Ferries in March 1987. By any means she was a ship not up to Sealink standards and being laid up for a while probably explained the build-up of mussels in the seawater cooling pipes which was always a problem when ships were laid up in the Fal. It was not until on passage north that her faults really showed up.

The *Stena Sailer*. (Justin Merrigan)

Under the command of Captain Glynne Pritchard and with Richard Jones as Chief Officer and Hugh Farrell as Second Officer, the *Stena Sailer* left Falmouth at 14.00 on 17th March. As soon as Bridge control was taken, the ship started moving astern at a rate of knots – 'zero' on the port engine combinator was in fact 'one' astern! On the passage from Falmouth to Dublin there were various combinations of the four engines. Of the two British Polar engines on each shaft the four failed to work together for any length of time.

The ship arrived at Dun Laoghaire at 14.00 on 18th March in appalling weather with sleet blowing in horizontally through the side wheelhouse window. Having successfully berthed on the west side of St Michael's Pier, the pier master wanted the ship to go out again and try the berth stern first. No chance! Departure for Holyhead was at 18.15 which was safely reached before midnight.

The following day brought fun and games; shifting around the Inner Harbour at Holyhead in NW 35 knots of wind with dud engines! During the initial shift from the Refit Berth to the Admiralty Pier, the wind kept blowing the heaving lines back on board but a line was eventually sent ashore for'd. But then, every time an attempt was made to screw the stern in, the engineers would phone the bridge with a polite request to ease off because the engines were overheating! In the end the manoeuvre was abandoned and it was decided to go outside to swing and come back into the Inner Harbour for the Refit Berth.

Captain Hugh Farrell. (Justin Merrigan)

It was in the final stages of this approach that the Chief Engineer appeared on the bridge, his face black with soot, with white rivulets of sweat running down his cheeks, saying, "We've got to stop the engines, the exhausts are glowing cherry red, can you anchor here?" And anchor they did, right in the middle of the Inner Harbour, off the Refit Berth, until the engines cooled sufficiently to allow normal berthing to continue!

SAILING ON RAILS

Captain Hugh Farrell

In 1977 the *St Columba* was considered the largest vessel possible for the Inner Harbour at Holyhead, being purpose built at Aalborg for British Rail, the port and the crossing to Dun Laoghaire. Berthing at the head of the harbour alongside the railway station on the east side of the port she dominated the scene being surrounded on three sides, her only way out being stern first through the middle of the harbour before going first around Turkeyshore corner and then around the Mail Pier dolphin and out into the space of the Outer Harbour to swing her bows seaward.

Having served on the *St Columba* for many years as deck officer, I eventually gained command of the ship in 1991 when under the Sealink Stena Line flag as the *Stena Hibernia*. I was not long in the role as her Night Master when I had the first of some challenging situations every ferry Master must undoubtedly face during the course of a career.

Under the command of the Day Master and my good friend Captain Richard Jones, later creator of the famous 'Bwana Swing', the ship had arrived with the 08.45 sailing from Dun Laoghaire on an October afternoon

The *Stena Hibernia*. (Justin Merrigan)

◀ The *Brian Boroime* ploughing into a gale. (W. Owen Williams)

▼ The *Holyhead Ferry I*. (Captain Walter Lloyd Williams)

in 1991 with a bad weather warning in operation. In the face of a northeast gale Richard was prudent and delayed the 14.45 sailing while awaiting a moderation in conditions. Meanwhile, the *Stena Cambria* was inward from Dun Laoghaire with Captain Tudor Jones and Night Master Captain John McClymont on board.

The *Stena Cambria* was three years younger than the *Stena Hibernia* and while the latter was a beautiful ship to handle, the former Dover vessel enjoyed more power in the bow thrust and was therefore a little easier to handle in marginal conditions. Thus, she was able to enter the Inner Harbour at the end of her crossing from Dun Laoghaire, but with us still at the Station she was forced to go alongside the Refit Berth and await our eventual departure, the alternative berth at Salt Island being untenable in the conditions.

Richard had kindly allowed me to remain in bed beyond the watch

Busy Dun Laoghaire: *St Columba*, *Dalriada*, *Duke of Lancaster*. (Kenneth Whyte)

changeover later that evening, being of the view that there was no point in everybody being up and about while the sailing was uncertain. With winds of Force 9 to 10 an attempt to sail with the 03.15 departure was made, using an offing line run over to the opposite berth from the port quarter but all attempts to screw her off were unsuccessful.

By first light I was now on the bridge after a reasonable night's sleep. The wind had moderated not a great deal, but perhaps enough to have another go. Having been up for 20 hours, Richard explained the situation and said he would remain on the bridge while I took her out.

Looking down the harbour from the bridge wing, and seeing the *Stena Cambria* on the Refit Berth, I knew if I was going to do this I could not hang around and so I discussed my options with Richard and another good friend and Senior Chief Engineer, the late Richard Hughes. Again, the offing rope would be used to help the stern out while screwing off. Turning to our Chief I asked him how much power I could give and as always with Richard every reassurance was given. "You give her everything you need Hugh, we'll give you what she'll take, everything we can."

Having selected Terry Dundee as the Quartermaster to take the wheel he joined Richard Jones and me in the aft wheelhouse as we prepared for departure (purpose-built Holyhead ships had an after bridge for astern navigation from the port). It now just remained for me to alert the *Stena Cambria* at the Refit Berth. Speaking to Captain Tudor Jones I told him we were going to have a go and if we could lift her off the berth we wouldn't be hanging around. I recall telling him, "I won't say I'll come out like a cork out of a champagne bottle, but we won't be hanging around!" Having received confirmation that the *Stena Cambria*'s lines were all secure, we rang for After Bridge Control on the telegraphs.

Heaving the bow out into position we then screwed the stern out while pulling on the stern offing rope. With engines working hard and a great deal of black smoke from the funnel we got the stern clear of the linkspan and into position. Letting go forward, it was then the turn of the offing rope and without any hesitation the combinator handles were swiftly placed on 10s – full astern both engines. The ship responded instantly, tracking down the middle of the harbour in the ideal position, so perfectly it seemed she was on rails! Passing the *Stena Cambria* with a good turn of speed, her crew and inward passengers could be seen waving with glee as they could now proceed to the station berth for disembarkation.

Having successfully got her off the berth, the next challenge was getting her around Turkeyshore corner and through 'The Gut', the pathing wind passing from one quarter of the ship to the other but she came around in perfect position continuing smartly to come around the Mail Pier dolphin before moving out into the swinging position. I kept further to the east for this due to the wind and the swing was completed safely. Ordering "Change Bridges, hard-a-starboard, full ahead", Richard, Terry and I quickly made our way to the main bridge to take over from the Chief Officer.

As we rounded the end of Holyhead's breakwater we reflected that the old girl had left the Inner Harbour as if on rails, but then she *was* built for the Railways!

THE BWANA SWING

Captain Richard Jones

Strong southerly gales always made departure from Holyhead's Station Berth stern first extremely difficult. As the *Stena Hibernia* lacked the power of the *Stena Cambria* in such conditions it became apparent to me that if we on the former *St Columba* failed to sail then the 'Cambria' might have to wait outside the port until the weather moderated.

After studying the charts for many a long hour and visiting the Container Terminal, I realised that by landing the stern of the ship and pinning it on one set of piles on the container berth there was just sufficient space to swing the ship there, allowing us to proceed out of the harbour bow first.

Captain Richard Jones. (Justin Merrigan)

At the time I was sailing as Night Master with Captain Ian Farrell as the Day Master. I think I had been talking to him for some time about the possibility of this manoeuvre when one day it was blowing a strong gale from the south. The Refit Berth was occupied, the *Stena Cambria* was outside the port with nowhere to go and I was in bed while Ian was preparing for the afternoon sailing. The next thing I was put on the shake as I was wanted on the bridge where I was told, "This is your bloody idea, so we'll do it together."

After a bit of a conflab we put the idea into practice and lo and behold the birth of the 'Bwana Swing'.

Over time this method was much improved upon but it could only be performed if tidal conditions were right and as the piles on the Container Berth were somewhat small, landing and keeping the stern on them was quite tricky. Although the container service had finished, the cranes were still in position which on a few occasions nearly caused the old adrenalin to flow! I am not sure how many Masters used this manoeuvre – Captain Ian Farrell and I did it regularly and Captain Hugh Farrell did it at least a couple of times.

And the name 'Bwana'? Before joining the Holyhead ships I was working as a surveyor in West Africa, so I was named 'Dick Bwana' by some wag on the *Slieve Donard*. Actually, the title 'Bwana' is from East Africa, but what the hell – Holyhead folk have never allowed a few thousand miles of geographical error to stand in the way of a good nickname!

RAILS ON THE IRISH SEA!

Captain Ray Veno

I found myself in the elderly train ferry *Cambridge Ferry* in February 1991, the ship having been called to Holyhead for emergency relief duties. My only recollection of her really is that I suppose somebody loved the ship somewhere!

The weather for the period she was in Holyhead was reasonable, the strongest being SW 7 at sea, quieter inside. I recall that berthing was awkward at times, there being no bow thrust; aim at the end of the pier and hope the shore gang were not dilatory in grabbing the heaving lines. They were used to having them 'delivered' into their hands from the ship, in a

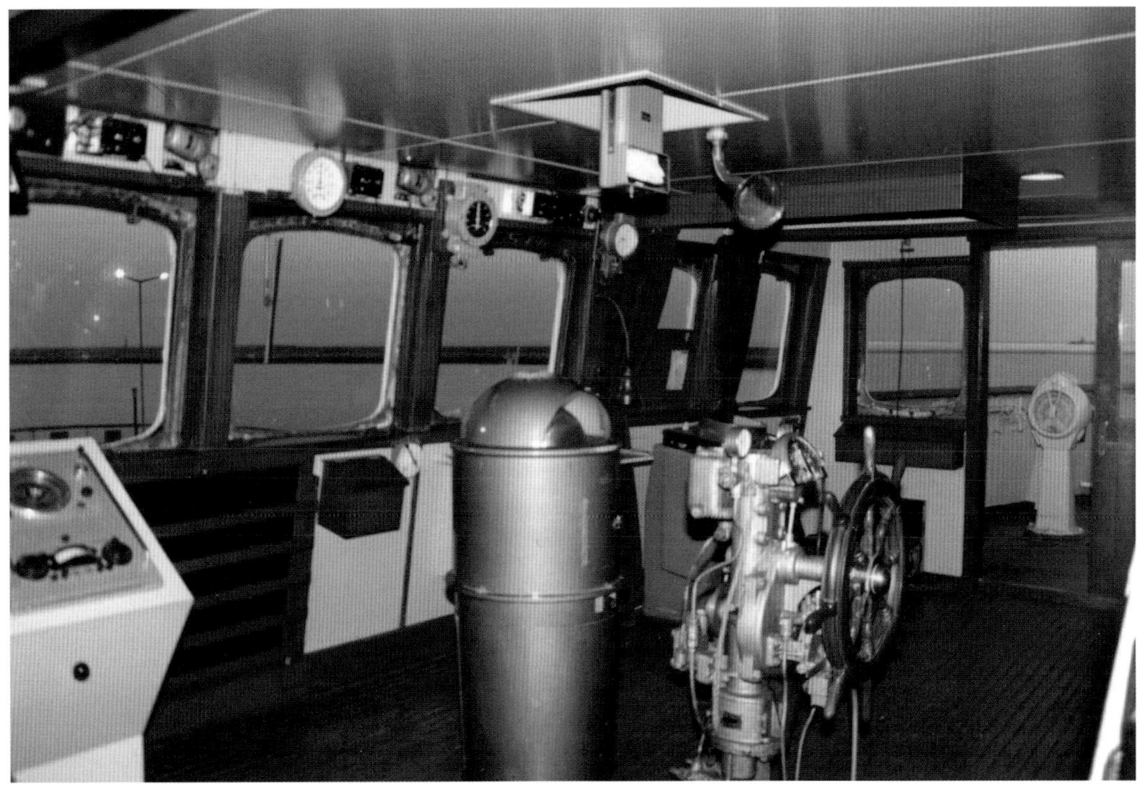

The wheelhouse of the *Cambridge Ferry*. (Justin Merrigan)

With the *Earl William* fitting out at the Refit Berth, the *Duke of Lancaster* rests at Holyhead's Boathouse Berth between Dun Laoghaire sailings. Captain John Bakewell remembers well this steamer. "I was in command of the *Duke of Lancaster* for a few weeks when she was on relief duty in Holyhead. Backing out of Holyhead was fine as she steered beautifully with her bow rudder. However, when proceeding ahead she was terrible to steer. The rudder didn't look much bigger than a dinner plate! Sailing into Holyhead, one had to put the rudder hard over somewhere by the North Stack in order to get her round the breakwater! Then getting her into the Inner Harbour caused many a grey hair!" (Kenneth Whyte)

manner of speaking. We were blown off on one occasion and it was time consuming screwing the bow/stern into the pier, there were no boats as I recall to run ropes for us.

In Holyhead, I went to the Station Berth with her using the small tug *Francis* on two occasions and swung inside on departure. The rest of the time at Holyhead I backed into Salt Island, always with a tug in attendance as I couldn't take a chance in the confines of the Gut. Departure was easy, screw off and away you go, no tug required.

At Dun Laoghaire, the west side of St Michael's Pier was a bit awkward but not dangerous at berthing and again there were no boats available to run ropes. I dropped anchor on one occasion and kedged her bow in to prevent landing heavily as there was no other way to stop her.

I was a very happy man the morning I was called to the phone at Dun Laoghaire's Carlisle Pier and told by our route director, Captain Peter

The *Lord Warden* arrives at Holyhead's station berth with Red Ensign lowered in respect for Lord Mountbatten. August 1979. This was this well-loved steamer's final year in service. Built in 1952 she was England's first purpose built stern loading car ferry. In the twilight of her career she opened a shortlived service between Fishguard and Dun Laoghaire in 1978, but it was at Holyhead that she saw out her Sealink career. (Kenneth Whyte)

McGowan, to remain tied up in the Irish port until Captain Dunlop arrived from Scotland later that morning. I then took her up to the Stranraer where he put her alongside.

Another daft thing was a clunking sound coming from the locking mechanism of the Admiralty safe in the Master's bedroom when the ship moved in a seaway; you couldn't do anything about it as it was enclosed in the door! So it was a settee job for a kip on night passage if you felt so inclined.

Released at Fishguard by the chartered *Stena Normandica* the *Avalon* saw out her Sealink career as a Holyhead ship. Here she is in 1980, her final year, moving into position off the Welsh port's station berth before letting go and moving stern first down the harbour. (Kenneth Whyte)

The *Slieve Donard* loads at Holyhead for her regular sailing to Dublin. Captain John Bakewell recalls one of his first trips as Master on the *Slieve Donard.* "With Glynne Pritchard as my Chief Officer, we arrived at night in Holyhead's Boathouse berth with a heavier landing than I would have liked! So we went down the gangway to see if any damage had been done. We couldn't see any damage to the ship but there was a strong smell of burning. I thought that we couldn't have slid along the piles that much for them to burn. The smell got stronger when suddenly I found that my coat pocket was on fire from my pipe!" (Captain Walter Lloyd Williams)

The *Great Western*
(John Hendy Collection)

Fishguard

A COW IN THE ENGINE ROOM

David Barwell

During my career as a marine engineer I had many unusual messages and reports from Chief Engineers over the years but one in particular I remember very well. I had just joined the Western Region of British Railways, (before the formation of Sealink) as the Superintendent Marine Engineer at Fishguard and was phoned early one morning by the Chief Engineer of the *Great Western* after she had just arrived in Fishguard Harbour.

The phone message went as follows: "Good morning Mr Barwell, this is the Chief Engineer of the *Great Western* speaking. I have to report that I have a cow in the engine room and I am wondering what I should do with it."

I resisted the temptation to suggest that he could try milking it and told him that I would be right down to sort it out!

The *Great Western* was in fact running a service between Waterford and Fishguard carrying live cattle 'on the hoof' from Ireland to the UK. On arrival in Fishguard, the animals were rested for several hours in a lairage at Fishguard before onward transport by road or rail, to farms in the UK for fattening.

On this occasion it had been a rough passage and the cow had jumped out of its pen, sauntered along the cattle deck, found the engine room door open and walked in to the top platform. It then fell down the stairs between the engines and the first thing that confronted the engineer on watch was a cow walking towards him.

When I arrived on the ship, the only thing to do was to humanely destroy the poor animal and lift it out of the engine room.

All in a marine engineer's daily routine!

THE *AVALON*'S FINEST HOUR

Brian Cleare

The *Avalon* came to us from Harwich on 15th July 1975 having been converted to a stern-loading car ferry at the end of her classic service on the North Sea. As built in 1963 she was the pride of the British Railways fleet. The conversion cost £1.75 million and involved the stripping of her main and lower decks to provide two car decks.

The *Avalon*'s fo'c'sle.
(Kenneth Whyte)

Undoubtedly, the *Avalon*'s finest hour came while on passage from Rosslare on the night of 8th February 1977. At 23.00 she received a call for assistance from the 1,500-ton Panamanian-flagged cattle carrier *El Tambo*, on fire off St David's on the Pembrokeshire coast.

The *El Tambo* had earlier been at Fishguard for ten days with engine trouble and was now on passage from Greenore to Tripoli with 917 head of cattle. With her engine room ablaze she sent out a distress call which was picked up by the *Avalon* and at 24 knots we rushed to her aid. We sighted the ship at 23.25 and by 23.43 were stopped two cables away from the casualty. With the *El Tambo*'s lifeboats on fire our Master, Captain Hubert Cooney, ordered the launching of one of our lifeboats to take the crew off the stricken ship.

Our Chief Officer, Norman Brown, who in later years would be Senior

The *Avalon*. (Kenneth Whyte)

Master of the *Felicity*, commanded our lifeboat, with myself among the crew. We took 21 crew members off the burning ship and brought them to the welcoming safety of the *Avalon*. Meanwhile, the oil-rig tanker *Arctic Sea* was racing to the scene from Milford Haven. When she arrived, we in the lifeboat passed a line between the two ships and the *El Tambo* was taken in tow. It was at this point that the *El Tambo*'s senior officers asked to be returned to their ship and having been brought across by our lifeboat they were joined by a fire-fighting party from HMS *Herald* which had now also arrived.

The excitement over, the *Avalon* was stood down and we resumed passage to Fishguard where we arrived a little over 2.5 hours behind schedule. The crew were made as comfortable as possible on board the *Avalon* until the Panamanian authorities could finalise arrangements. The *El Tambo* herself was towed to Fishguard where she eventually sank at her moorings and was broken up. As for the cattle – they were safely transferred to other ships.

The *Avalon*.
(Don Smith/Pictureships)

Weymouth

FIRE IN THE *AILSA PRINCESS*

Captain Martin Scott

I was Master of the *Ailsa Princess* when we had a potentially serious fire on Saturday 24th July 1982.

We were approaching the inner harbour at Cherbourg at about 14.00 French time when flames were reported from the car deck. Approximately 350 passengers had already boarded their coaches prior to disembarkation. Jim Herring, the Chief Officer, gathered as many deck crew together as possible and disappeared into the car deck. Apparently the flames were coming from a caravan on the port side forward of the lower car deck. The coach passengers were quickly brought back up into the accommodation and attempts were made to extinguish the fire.

The *Ailsa Princess*.
(John Hendy)

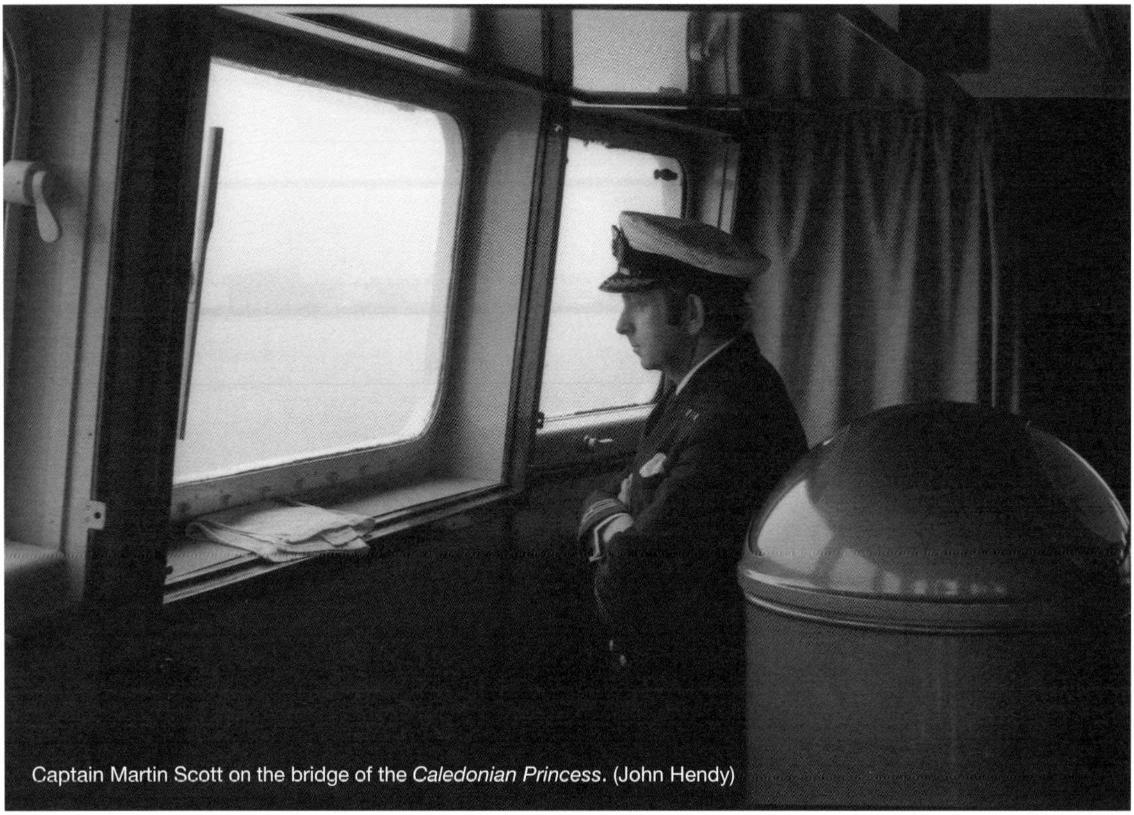

Captain Martin Scott on the bridge of the *Caledonian Princess*. (John Hendy)

▶ Welcome to Jersey! The service to Cherbourg was just one of a network of Sealink western Channel routes. From Weymouth and Portsmouth there were also links to Jersey and Guernsey latterly operated by the *Earl Godwin*, *Earl William*, *Earl Granville* and the *Earl Harold* (ex-*Ailsa Princess*). (John Hendy)

Meanwhile, with me and the radio officer on the bridge and a couple of the crew fore and aft, the *Ailsa Princess* was made fast alongside her normal berth. Jim was having trouble controlling the flames within and around the caravan so the car deck sprinkler system was activated. Initially we had turned off the main car deck fans but as this had merely caused the accommodation to start filling with smoke, we decided to start them up again. Apparently the smoke coming from the ventilators was most impressive to those ashore!

We decided to get all the passengers ashore and Leslie Webb, the Purser, with the efficiency of a regimental sergeant-major soon had our 900 passengers safely onto the jetty via the main passenger gangway.

The fire continued to burn fiercely and though attempts were made to open the bow door to allow the Cherbourg fire brigade onto the scene, this was not possible as electrical circuits had been damaged. A local tug kindly sprayed water on the port side of our hull which was by now glowing red in parts.

Cars were stowed above and around the caravan in question and at this

The *Falaise* launched car ferry services from Weymouth to the Channel Islands in 1973. Boiler trouble brought a sudden halt to her career in 1974 and after layup at Holyhead she was sold for scrap in December 1974.
(Don Smith/Pictureships)

Summer at Weymouth with the *Earl Godwin* resting between Channel Islands sailings while the *Maid of Kent* loads for Cherbourg. (Kenneth Whyte)

stage I was merely waiting for the petrol tanks to brew up so the rest of us could swiftly go ashore for a good lunch. It was somewhat surreal to see all our passengers at the end of the jetty in a silent mass watching the show.

Eventually, the combination of the sprinkler system and the firefighters' efforts quenched the flames. Surprisingly, and thankfully, no petrol tanks exploded but the caravan was reduced to a charred framework. The car deck sprinkler systems had obviously helped contain the fire and after getting the bow visor open, passengers were finally able to drive most of their cars away without damage. However, approximately half a dozen were not going to be driven to the South of France that day.

Our UK-bound passengers were accommodated with Townsend Thoresen and we made our own way back to Weymouth. Surprisingly, damage to the ship's hull was negligible but it took us many months to get rid of the smoke damage to the paint, especially the deckheads.

It was surprising to find the whole incident had only taken three hours, docking in Weymouth at 20.00 that night. Pats on the back all round were duly received from Captain Jack Watt, the Chief Marine Superintendent!

BEATING THE CHERBOURG BLOCKADE

Captain Martin Scott

The day to day routine of life on board a ferry can occasionally become a little dull although the events of 19th July 1984 certainly livened things up a bit.

When we arrived at Cherbourg in the *Ailsa Princess*, we found all three ramps blocked by Spanish lorries and the local French authorities seemingly unwilling to assist us.

We were carrying 300 holidaymakers and about 60 cars and it very much looked as if a return to Weymouth was on the cards. Fortunately, it was coming up to high water and we thought we had a chance of saving the situation by dropping our stern ramp straight onto a vacant quay.

We measured our ramps and the clearance at high tide and thought that we could make it between noon and 13.30. We got the passengers together and told them what we planned to do. They were all for it although we didn't want to make our plans too obvious in case the lorry drivers got wind of it and tried to prevent us.

The *Earl Godwin*. (John Hendy)

At the appointed time, I took the 'Ailsa' out into the middle of the harbour and swung her stern through ninety degrees to the empty quay before lowering the stern ramp. We had about a foot of clearance. The engines were on for about an hour and a half and the thrusters started to overheat. We used the anchor and ropes to hold the vessel and the ramp onto the quay wall although the ropes were taking a tremendous strain but luckily we didn't have anything big on board. Just to complicate matters, a nasty little wind then blew up.

We pulled away at 13.34 with 300 new passengers, 30 cars and 30 caravans. It was quite a relief but it was the only way to do it. The *Ailsa Princess* eventually arrived back at Weymouth about seven hours late.

Editor's note: Captain Scott was warmly praised by Michael Edwards (Sealink's Assistant Manager at Weymouth) who congratulated him on "a remarkable feat of seamanship".

How it used to be on board the *Maid of Kent*'s Promenade Deck (Kenneth Whyte)

Isle of Wight

PAYING RESPECTS!

Dave Rowland

Around 1982, it would appear that one of the old hands had gone to that great dry dock in the sky. I'd never met the chap, it was years before my time, but it appears that he'd always expressed a wish to have his ashes scattered from a Portsmouth to Ryde ferry.

Enquiries had apparently been made and the idea had been given the go-ahead. The scattering was arranged for a quiet time on a Tuesday; our Master, the late Captain Chris Javes, was more than obliging. The ship, either the *Brading* or *Southsea*, would slow right down after passing the West Sturbridge buoy, about a mile off the end of Ryde Pier and he would then turn her so that the port side would be downwind, in order to prevent a disaster. A couple of the crew would open up the port side sponson doors and stand respectfully either side (actually they needed to be there to hold the doors open); the grieving entourage would then do the deed, say a few words, then retire to the bar to toast their old colleague.

The Master was to allow a minute or two before resuming the course to Ryde. Came the day, and all went swimmingly; a lovely, bright, calm day;

The *Southsea*. (John Faulkner)

perfect. All went well until the time came for the scattering of the ashes before the mourners suddenly became aware that no one had remembered to bring the urn. Lots of embarrassed coughs and appropriate jokes ensued and it was resolved to rearrange the whole thing again for the following week. Imagine; you arrange a funeral, and the body never bothers to show up...!

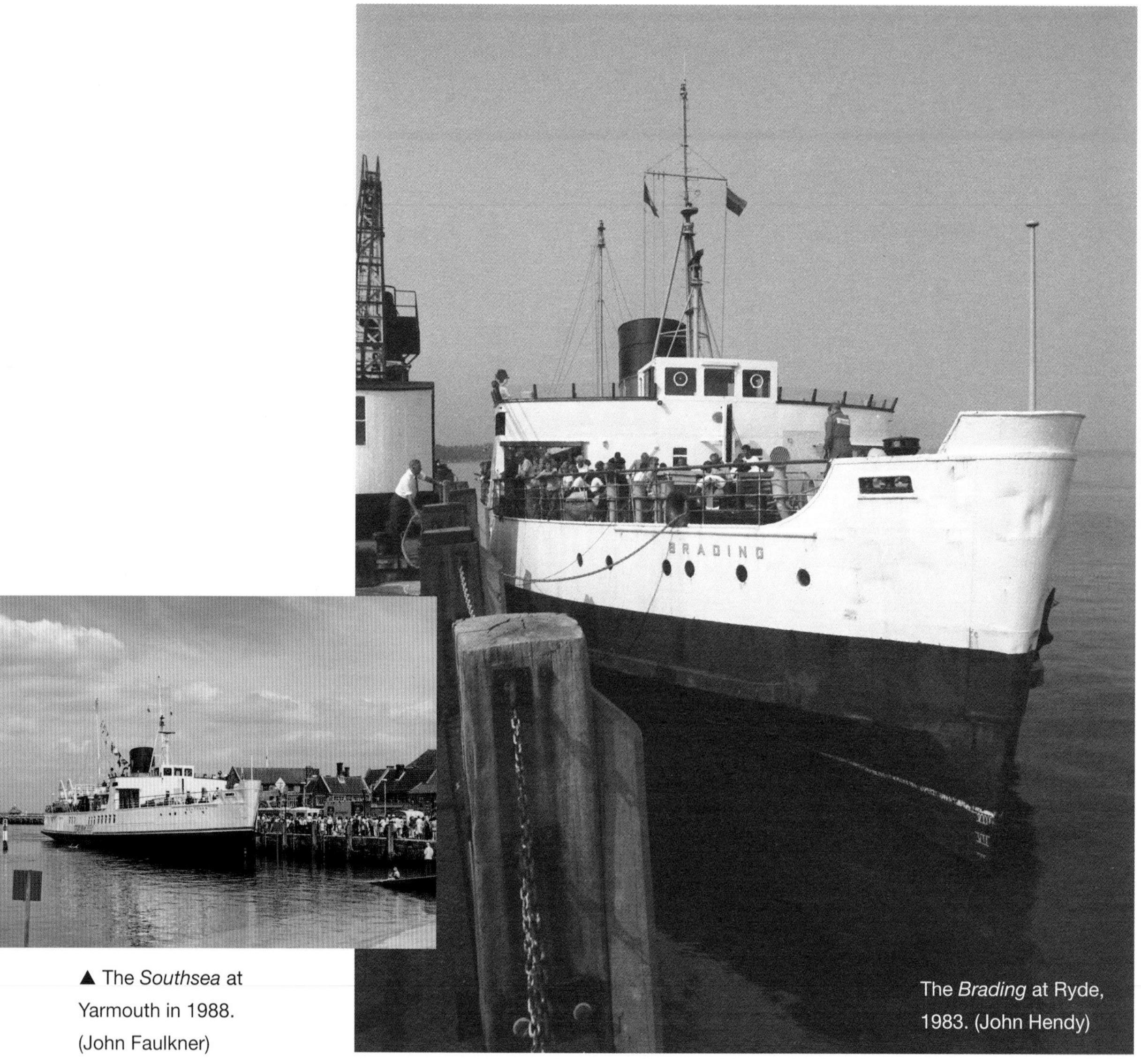

▲ The *Southsea* at Yarmouth in 1988. (John Faulkner)

The *Brading* at Ryde, 1983. (John Hendy)

Newhaven

NEWHAVEN RELIEF

Captain George Sutcliffe (Dover)

In the autumn of 1973 I had just been dropped back to 1st Officer on the *Anderida* at Dover for the winter when a request came from Newhaven for a Master with *Hengist* or *Horsa* experience to go down there to give some relief to the Masters of the newly arrived *Senlac*. They had sickness among the Masters which meant they were not getting any time off. None of our

The *Senlac* leaving Newhaven in 1974. (Don Smith/Pictureships)

The *Senlac*. (John Hendy)

masters were really interested although my experience of handling an H boat was to once take the *Hengist* out of Folkestone. I kept quiet and volunteered. It was another very interesting experience.

Until I had sufficient navigations in that port to get my pilotage exemption, I had a 1st Officer with me who already had his pilot licence. This officer was very worried when I first arrived as he saw me as a threat to his own promotion prospects. I soon reassured him that I had no intention of transferring to Newhaven permanently and I was only there until their Relief Master was fit to step in again.

The *Villandry*.
(John Hendy collection)

It was interesting in that Newhaven was steeped in traditional ways to a far greater degree than Dover which had benefitted from a large influx of officers from deep sea. One tradition, which I can claim to have made a small contribution to changing, was the use of 'swinging wires' in Dieppe. When you arrived, these wires were rigged aft so that when leaving they held the stern to the quay while the bow was swung to port around 90+ degrees. They were then let go and the ship had to swing through nearly 180 degrees to join the channel out. I felt that this made a lot of work and was unnecessary in view of the ship's handling characteristics. Before making any change I cut out a piece of card to represent the ship to the same scale as the Dieppe chart and swung that on the chart to make sure I had sufficient clearances. Then on my next arrival I gave the order 'no need to rig the swinging wires'. It was so unusual that the 2nd Officer came to my cabin and asked me if that was correct. When we left I eased the ship out of the berth sideways using bow thrust and propellers then swung her through 90 degrees to exit the port.

I hardly think I endeared myself to the Senior Master for introducing such a revolutionary manoeuvre with his ship. It just seemed to make sense to me as it saved the awkward work of rigging the wires and saved time and fuel turning the ship through 90 degrees as opposed to 270 degrees.

On arrival back from Newhaven I found that the Staff Office were regarding me more as a Master who had on occasions dropped back to 1st Officer as opposed to being a 1st Officer who was lucky to get the chance to go out as Master.

The *Maid of Kent* laid up at Newhaven in October 1965. (John Hendy)

SEALINK TO THE RESCUE

Justin Merrigan

As a schoolboy keenly interested in ships, and in particular the Sealink fleet, I always looked forward to receiving my copy of the company's in-house magazine 'Sealink News' in the post. I really did feel part of the Sealink family, always being made so welcome on board the ships in my home port of Dun Laoghaire and to be included on the mailing list for this excellent magazine was a huge source of enjoyment.

Contained within the covers of 'Sealink News' was all the latest from around the fleet and often this contained such adventures of responses to distress calls by Sealink ships going about their normal routines.

One such incident involved the *Senlac* on passage between Newhaven and Dieppe on 3rd July 1978 and under the command of Captain Paul Levesley. At 19.02 the ship received a distress call from the *Arosette*, a German vessel of 499 tons, bound for Shoreham with a cargo of steel in her hold and timber on her deck. The *Senlac* arrived on scene at 19.23 to find the *Arosette* at her angle of loll with a starboard list of 45-50 degrees. A rough sea and force 7 wind had probably caused the timber to absorb a substantial amount of water, making the vessel unstable. Accordingly, she radioed that she needed an axe to free her foredeck lashings.

With the *Senlac* providing a lee for the *Arosette*, line-throwing apparatus was used and the axe was passed over; subsequently one of the German's crew members ventured on deck and cut the lashings. Attempts were made to pass other gear by this method but most of it ended up in the water.

By this time, Newhaven Lifeboat had arrived and with the *Senlac* making a lee for her she closed with the casualty's. However, it soon became obvious that a tug was required and Sealink's *Meeching* was summoned from Newhaven. With the deck cargo nearly gone the *Arosette* requested the *Senlac* to expose her to the weather to allow the sea to wash off the remaining wood.

On the arrival of the *Meeching* the *Senlac* was stood down and proceeded on passage at 21.25. The standard of seamanship to keep a vessel such as the *Senlac* in a position from which assistance could be rendered was not the easiest job in the world, particularly with a rough sea.

▲ The wheelhouse of the *Earl Leofric*. (John Hendy)

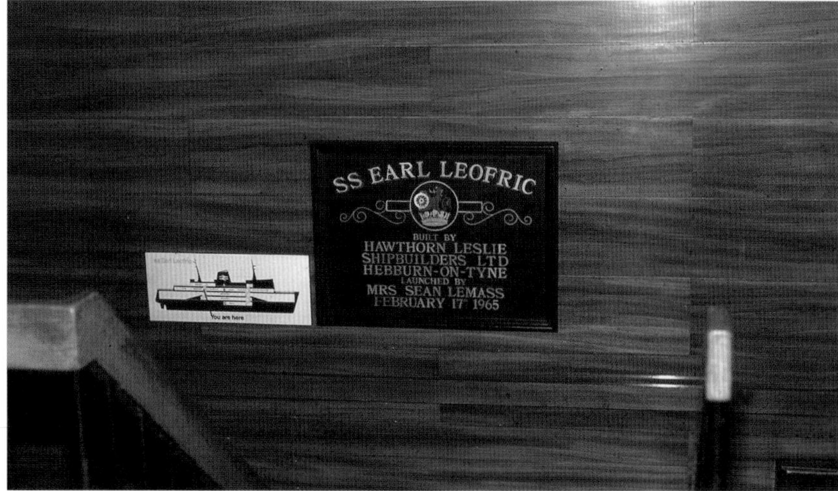

▶ The *Earl Leofric* was launched by the wife of the Irish Taoiseach as the *Holyhead Ferry 1*. (Kenneth Whyte)

Dover and Folkestone

THE SEALINK FLEET CONVERTED TO BURN HEAVY FUEL OIL

David Barwell (former Superintendent Engineer in Chief)

Between the years 1971 and 1974 the price of fuel increased by a factor of four which had a significant effect on the profitability of Sealink shipping services which operated motor ships burning diesel oil. As a consequence, the engineering department started to investigate the possibility of converting its fleet of motor ships, (which used medium speed diesel engines for main

The *Hengist*.
(Don Smith/Pictureships)

The *Horsa*.
(Don Smith/Pictureships)

propulsion) to burn heavy fuel oil (HFO) instead of diesel. The price of heavy fuel oil in 1974 was approximately 65 per cent that of diesel and that price differential has been maintained to the present day. The current price of HFO at say Rotterdam is 615 dollars per metric tonne compared to 950 dollars for diesel.

It had been the practice for many years on deep sea going vessels to burn HFO both on large bore diesel engines, and also in medium speed engined vessels but the procedure on deep sea going ships was to use a 'mixing tank' arrangement where the engines burnt diesel oil to start and to manoeuvre in port and then slowly changed over to heated HFO on passage, a procedure which took at least an hour after 'full away'. On arrival at the destination port, deep sea vessels would revert to diesel oil one hour before arrival. Such a procedure on a ferry, with passage times between say two and four hours is impracticable, and it follows that if a ferry is to operate on HFO it has to run, start and manoeuvre on it. In layman's terms, an engine burning HFO on a ferry never sees another drop of diesel oil for the whole of its operating life.

The conversion to burn HFO involved a number of system design changes. Obviously the fuel supply (IFO 180 centistokes) to the main engines has to be heated to say 115 degrees centigrade and continuously re-circulated back to the daily service tank. The engine cooling system has to be modified to also heat the engine to operating temperature before starting the engines. All bunker tanks and the daily service tank must be fitted with heating coils and the fuel supply from the bunker tanks to the daily service tank must pass through a centrifugal separator.

The first ship to be converted to burn HFO was the *Hengist* of 1972 operating on the Folkestone to Boulogne service and all that I can really say about the changeover was that it was an unqualified success. The vessel operated quite normally; the ship's engineers quickly adjusted to the changed operating procedures, there was no noticeable visible change in the smoke emissions from the funnel and, in the long term surprisingly, there was no increase in required engine maintenance work. Subsequent experience has verified that exhaust valve life and cylinder liner wear are very little different than when operating on diesel fuel although a higher grade of lubricating needs to be used.

Following on from the successful conversion of the *Hengist* and her sister *Horsa* the rest of the fleet was converted to burn HFO; each conversion being undertaken in the normal overhaul period on each ship.

The conversion of the Sealink fleet to burn HFO for main engine propulsion resulted in a major improvement in the profitability of each of the Sealink's routes. I think it is also true to say that most major European ferry operators followed Sealink's example and converted their fleets to burn HFO.

THE GREAT STORM – OCTOBER 1987
THE *HENGIST* AGROUND

Dave Tyler

All seemed well when I joined the *Hengist* at Folkestone harbour at the customary time of 06.45 to commence a 24-hour turn of duty; which comprised three return crossings to the French port of Boulogne and back, followed by a lay-by period of six hours back in Folkestone, before the next crew joined at 06.45 the following day to take over. Little did we know what lay in store for us as events would unfold over the next few hours.

After carrying routine checks to essential plant and equipment we departed Folkestone punctually at 07.45 to take up our regular service. Over the course of the day weather conditions slowly but surely deteriorated, causing delay and disruption to the many ferries and other vessels plying

The *Hengist* ashore. (John Hendy)

their trade in the channel that day. Despite the conditions and a report on BBC television that there was even a suggestion that we would experience hurricane force winds later that day we were not unduly concerned. Particularly given that the threat of a hurricane had been dismissed by the BBC weather forecaster; a remark that would come back to haunt him!

As the day progressed we were increasingly chasing our tail in a vain endeavour to keep some sort of normality to our timetable which was falling behind. Little did we realise to quite what extent the *Hengist*'s schedule would be disrupted over the coming winter months.

In fact as we completed our second return crossing of the day to berth back into Folkestone, conditions had deteriorated to such a degree that it took almost four hours for the Master, Captain Sid Bridgewater to manoeuvre the vessel alongside the quay and disembark our cargo of ashen-faced passengers and freight. All of this was taking place under the nose of the company chairman/owner Mr James Sherwood who was travelling with us

The *Hengist* ashore. (Dave Tyler)

▶ The *Hengist* ashore.
(Dave Tyler)

▼ The *Hengist* ashore.
(Dave Tyler)

at the time, having embarked earlier that afternoon in Boulogne.

As we were now several hours behind schedule the resulting delay put the *Hengist* so hopelessly behind our timetable that the decision was taken, in the light of various factors; mainly the worsening weather, to cancel our final round trip of the shift and to lay-by for the night, prior to resuming normal service the following day.

One of the reasons behind our difficulties in berthing in Folkestone that night was due to fact the vessel's bow thrust propulsion unit was not available. This was because one of the *Hengist*'s three main generating sets had been dismantled and was undergoing repairs following a mechanical failure. A temporary replacement generator had been provided which was welded in place on the funnel deck. However, this could not be paralleled with the two remaining operational generators and was solely used to service the vessel's bow thrust/propulsion unit. There were problems with the temporary generator rendering non-operational and which subsequently necessitated the attendance of a service engineer from its manufacturer.

Once the passengers and freight had disembarked, the vessel moved out of the ramp and proceeded down the quay to the forward lay-by berth. The manning/crewing level was set at status level Category Two; leaving a reduced crew which would be sufficient to take the ship out to sea should it be necessary.

As the night wore on, the wind speed increased to almost hurricane force. The tide rose, exposing the *Hengist* to the increasing wind speeds and subsequent sea conditions so that our mooring ropes and lines were parting with increased regularity and it became nigh on impossible to keep the ship in the berth. As if this wasn't bad enough, she was getting damaged due to the swell as she was continually buffeted against the quay. It was therefore decided to proceed out to sea, the idea being to ride out the storm.

In the conspicuous absence of the shore force, one of the *Hengist*'s deck crew went ashore to untie us. With this task completed we headed out to sea, to ride the storm, only to within a very short space of time, encounter a wave with enough strength to cause us to pitch and roll so violently that the rotor which had been removed from the dismantled main generating set undergoing repairs, broke adrift from its restraining ropes and smashed into one of the two operational generators. Consequently, this disabled one of the generators and thus transferred the *Hengist*'s whole electrical load onto the last remaining generator, causing to it trip its overload load safety device and shut down.

This had the knock-on effect of shutting down both main engines and steering gear. We were now without engines, electrical power or steering ability and at the mercy of the waves. What was it that weather forecaster said on the BBC about there being no hurricane coming up the Channel tonight?

Being without main power, I went up to the boat deck to check the emergency generator which provided power to essential circuits only. As I went out on to the Boat Deck all I could hear was the wind screaming like a high-pitched whistle; I had never heard anything like it before or since, thank goodness.

I went back down to the engine control room to assist the Chief and Second Engineer in attempting to start the main engines, all to no avail as we were rolling so violently from side to side that the main engine low lube oil safety devices kept activating, thus preventing the engines from starting.

Also on board that night and joining us in the engine control room was the service engineer from the temporary generator manufacturer. The poor chap had never been on a ship before in his life and said he thought it would be "rough out here, but not this bad". Naturally, we told him this was the norm; his face was a picture.

We continued trying to re-start the engines as we rolled and pitched in an unpredictable fashion, but it was hopeless, I watched as the four-drawer filing cabinet containing the technical library, instruction manuals and the like just fell over on its side, narrowly missing the Second Engineer, as the vessel was thrown about at the mercy of the waves.

At one stage I was only able to stand upright, by virtue of holding onto a handrail that was located horizontally along the length of the centre section of the main engines control console. I used to think that the handrail was overkill and unnecessary, but quickly formed second thoughts that night.

Eventually, having lost all track of time, our movement seemed to reduce to more of a rocking motion. At this point Captain Bridgewater rang down, instructing us to evacuate the engine room and muster outside of the officer's accommodation on the Boat Deck collecting our life jackets on the way. There we met up with the remaining crew members and all sat there together; sitting was far safer than standing.

At last we stopped rocking, relief? Yes, but we were aground! Unfortunately we didn't know where, it being pitch black outside and with widespread power cuts across the region.

After the vessel grounded we made are our way up to the bridge, all 23 of us including the service engineer on his maiden voyage! As we stood there in the semi darkness with only the emergency lighting available, Captain

Bridgewater suggested that it may be an opportune time to say a prayer and I for one did not hesitate to take him up on his suggestion; I suspect that I was not alone. Later, Johnny Hopkins, the Purser that night, suggested that I christen my newly born daughter of eleven days, Gale!

As the sun came up and we could make out land, we could see that we were lodged high and dry on a concrete groyne, which formed part of the promenade adjacent to the Warren area east of Folkestone. A comforting sight if ever I saw one. As we looked around to get our bearings we spotted a welcoming party; HM Customs and Excise waiting in their vehicle, they certainly did not waste any time in making their presence known.

What now? The air sea rescue helicopter based at Manston, Kent, offered to lift us off but this invitation was politely declined. We eventually left the vessel courtesy of the Kent Fire Brigade, who erected and secured a ladder to one of our passenger gangway doors.

A coach was waiting for us to take us back to Folkestone Harbour, where we retrieved our cars to make our way home. Driving home proved hazardous with many of the roads in East Kent closed with blown over trees strewn across them. I had to make a detour via Deal to get back to Thanet due to all the road closures but it was not until I drove past Northdown Park in Cliftonville, close to where I live and saw at least half of its huge trees lying flat, that I realised the extent and force of the wind that night. What was it that BBC weather forecaster had said again?

THE NIGHT OF THE GREAT STORM 2
THE *ST CHRISTOPHER*'S ESCAPE

Richard Broady

At the time I was a Foreign Exchange cashier on board the *St Christopher* under the command of Captain Colin Roberts. On that night we left Calais bound for Dover just after midnight – the weather was still and warm, we had approximately 90 passengers on board and the lower car deck was fully loaded – the top car deck was empty.

Once we left Calais, the sea started to get a bit lumpy and within about 30 minutes we were in a good old English Channel blow. I closed the exchange office – nobody wants to change money when they are being ill and went to the drivers' lounge for a beer and a chat. I had a radio scanner with me and as we sat there we heard a fishing vessel putting out a Mayday, shortly followed by the Mayday call from the *Hengist* – as we all knew the *Hengist* and her crew, it focused the attention a little bit.

About an hour after leaving Calais there was an enormous bang, and the

▲ Built in 1960 as the *Dover*, the stern loading car ferry was converted to drive through operations in 1977. Emerging as the *Earl Siward* she remained in service until replaced by the new *St Christopher* in 1981. (Kenneth Whyte)

▶ The *St Christopher* leaves Calais for Dover in November 1985. (John Hendy)

ferry tilted hard to starboard, everything slid across the lounge and ended up in a heap against a bulkhead, including some of the people in the lounge. In an instant the lights went out and we heard the engines stop and the sound of them trying to start. Somewhere on board a woman was screaming very loudly.

After a minute or two the engines restarted and the lights came back on – the lounge looked like a bomb had hit it, everything was smashed and in a pile.

It turned out that an abnormal wave had hit the upper bow door of the ferry and split it open like a piece of paper, the car decks were flooded as was the engine room, stalling the engines.

We were told afterwards that the ferry had listed 39 per cent and had even one car been on the top car deck it would have been enough to turn us over. As it was, the vehicles on the lower car deck were smashed to pieces; a lorry fell over on a VW camper van which ended up about 2ft high.

When we finally got to Dover at 02.15 the car deck had to be unloaded with fork lift trucks and cranes; it took three days.

(This article originally appeared on the BBC website)

A CLOSE SHAVE

Gerry Sutton

Many years back, while sailing as a Junior Engineer on the *St Patrick* based at Dover and Folkestone, a Chief Engineer was in the process of growing a full set of whiskers. He was very touchy about the progress of this beard and we were all warned that any remarks regarding it would not be tolerated.

However, I knew that one of our firemen (many years at sea, through the war etc. "I've rung more salt water from my socks than you've sailed on lad") would be unable to remain silent. One morning as he was climbing the ladder out of the Engine Room adjacent to the manoeuvring platform where the Chief was standing, he paused and said in a stage whisper to the Greaser standing by the Engine Room telegraph, "I see there's a strike at Gillettes!"

Result: gales of laughter all round and even the Chief had to join in – one nil to the Boiler Room!

I must mention the *St Patrick* – a ship that would roll on wet grass! There was only natural draught ventilation into the engine room. The Heavy Fuel oil and Diesel bunkers would get cross contamination and occasionally seawater would get in. The auxiliary machinery was a mix of reciprocating and turbo feed pumps – the Glennifer diesel generators were a nightmare. Regardless of all that she had character and I had some good

The *St Patrick*. (John Hendy)

times on her. She certainly made me appreciate the motor ships when they were introduced.

THE *HAMPTON FERRY* AND AN ACT OF DEFIANCE

Captain Peter Dunkley

I served with the Dover/Folkestone section of Sealink, or the Southern Region of British Railways as it was newly called when I joined in 1948. For the last ten years of my service – 1964-74 – I was Master of most of the good old ships; 'steam jobs' not clockwork boats, and one that comes to mind is the *Hampton Ferry* which I was privileged to take on her last trip.

She came off service about July 1969 when the *Vortigern* arrived, and was laid up at No.5 Admiralty Pier. Then one lovely day in August, I took her away from Dover, around the land to Holyhead to lay up for sale which, I believe, happened in November that year. It is a trip I shall never forget, because I am one of those nuts who think that ships have souls and I am

Captain Peter Dunkley sharing a yarn with Chief Engineer Gordon Hart in the engine room of the *Caesarea*. (John Hendy)

The *Hampton Ferry* at Holyhead. (Ian Collard)

sure that the old girl was determined not to go to Holyhead. We already had two out of four boilers shut down because of faulty tubes, so our speed was about 8 and an onion. Rounding the end of the land (Longships) the weather went bad on us, NW 7/8 and a heavy swell and, sure enough, one more of the boilers packed up. By some miracle, the engineers got it going again and we made Holyhead in pitch darkness. When daylight came and I saw where the pilot had brought us through, I nearly had a fit as I am sure you would have done too if you know Holyhead Harbour at low water. The pilot naturally was a Mr Jones, who brought his dog with him!

Later that day I took the ship to the buoys in the outer harbour and although it was calm and no wind, I had a devil of a job nudging her up to the buoy – a final act of defiance.

I was sad to leave her, as were most of the lads, but the good old *Shepperton Ferry* was still running and so I had some time in command of her. These were the good old days with ships like the *Lord Warden*, *Maid of Kent*, *Dinard* and the Folkestone cargo boats. The finest of all these ships, I think, was the *Canterbury*.

The *Shepperton Ferry*.

CAPTAIN JOHN ARTHUR AND THE *VORTIGERN*

John Hendy

The *Vortigern*'s first Senior Master was the late Captain John Arthur who transferred to her from the pre-war train ferry *Shepperton Ferry*. In those days the Senior Master in the fleet always took the 'Golden Arrow' passenger steamer *Invicta*, and the other passenger vessels *Maid of Orleans* (1949) and *St Patrick* (1948) were second and third in order of seniority. The older Masters preferred the traditional tried and tested ships and were not particularly interested in innovation.

John Arthur was then seventh in order of local seniority but the fact existed that none of those ahead of him were interested in the new ship and as he enjoyed both train ferries and the Dunkirk service and was always ready to rise to a challenge, he became the obvious choice for this prestigious appointment.

The £2.5 million *Vortigern* was not only BR's first diesel-driven vessel in the Dover Strait but she was also the first to have a bow visor and the first to be fitted with variable-pitch propellers and bow thrusters which Captain Arthur claimed would make the traditional bow-rudder superfluous.

John Arthur remained as the *Vortigern*'s Senior Master until taking command of the new *St Anselm* in 1980. At this time Captain Gerry Sutton became the ship's Senior Master and

Commodore John Arthur, brings the *St Anselm* out of Calais for the final time on his retirement day. (John Hendy)

he was in turn succeeded by Captain Mike Bodiam; previously Master of the *Caesarea* and then briefly of the *Caledonian Princess* during her 1981 stint on the Dover Strait.

Speaking with John Arthur years later about his days in the *Vortigern*, he freely admitted that she was 'great fun' and very much his 'toy'. He never lost interest in playing with her just to see what she could and could not do. Such was his confidence that he trained no fewer than 20 Masters in the ship.

Captain Arthur vividly remembered an early problem during trials, which commenced on 9th July 1969, concerning the filling of the ship's ballast tanks. A second tank was inadvertently filled by a surveyor which caused the vessel to settle in the bow and for a while all those on the bridge

The *Vortigern* at Boulogne in August 1977. (Don Smith/Pictureships)

believed that she was sinking. So serious was the perceived danger that Captain Arthur and the pilot were busy selecting sandy places on the coast where they could run the ship aground when the fault was discovered and quickly rectified.

Following successful trials, the *Vortigern* was finally delivered to the British Railways Board on 18th July. On her arrival at Dover from the Tyne on 26th July, the new ferry waited in the outer harbour for a berth on the Admiralty Pier to be vacated. Captain Arthur's old ship the *Shepperton Ferry* happened to be at anchor 'in the bay' and so he took his new command alongside in order to shout a conversation with her Master. Being unaware of the added manoeuvrability that bow thrusters and variable-pitch propellers provided, the 'Shepperton's' Captain was very concerned by this manoeuvre (as was the Marine Superintendent) but the *Vortigern* could turn on a sixpence and there was never any danger that the ships might collide. In fact she could hold herself still in winds of up to force 6.

Captain Arthur was one of the great characters of the Dover Sealink fleet.

Commodore John Arthur bringing the *St Anselm* alongside the Admiralty Pier on the occasion of her first trials arrival from Calais in October 1980. (John Hendy)

The *St Anselm* dressed overall for Commodore Arthur's retirement. (John Hendy)

He left the *Vortigern* to become Senior Master of the new-generation *St Anselm* in 1980, then being promoted to Fleet Commodore. He retired the following year after almost 39 years in local railway/Sealink service and sadly went aloft in 2008.

'MAKEE LEARN'

Captain George Sutcliffe

I joined British Railways, Southern Region in 1965 and the first ship I was sent to was the *Maid of Kent*. To my surprise I was told I was joining her as 'Makee Learn' 2nd Officer. This was new to me as when I was deep sea you were just appointed to a ship in a rank and expected to get on with it. I soon realised that the ferries had set routines that you had to learn if the job was to go smoothly. For instance, when you stood by aft to leave on a deep sea ship you didn't do anything until you were told to do so from the bridge. On the ferries once the gangway or ramp was out you immediately singled up and informed the bridge that you were ready; the next order was let go. Also, after sailing, when the 2nd Officer arrived on the bridge you had to be able to inform the Master of the course to set for the prevailing state of tide and on certain ships, the engine revolutions to set to maintain the correct arrival time. There were tables that had been compiled over the years to aid you to achieve this. It really was a service that was maintained by set routines which had been established over the years.

Captain George Sutcliffe. (Mary Sutcliffe)

I was most fortunate in that I had joined the company at a time when they had decided to no longer offer contracts to officers who did not hold a Master Foreign Going Certificate. This was well in advance of Government legislation which made it a requirement for Masters of the ferries to hold the higher qualification. There were several officers senior to myself who were not contracted and only held Master's Home Trade Certificates who decided there was no future for them on the ships and took up Berthing Master's positions or went to Companies that had not changed their requirements. As a result of this I was not laid off at the end of the Summer season and was offered a contract within a year or two.

My main impression of my time as 2nd Officer was of a feeling of freedom. Once you were clear of the port, the Master disappeared and the con was yours. This contrasted with deep sea where, once you were in restricted waters you were under constant supervision, or even had a pilot on board. Friends who were still deep sea used to say to me, "Don't you find it boring going back and forth across the ditch?" My reply was, "It is a lot less boring than a four-hour watch in mid-ocean."

Again due to my fortunate timing in joining the company, I very quickly found myself promoted to 1st Officer. Then, joy of joys, I was able to develop my abilities as a ship handler which I really did thoroughly enjoy, whatever

The *Maid of Orleans* leaving Dover in August 1973 (Don Smith/Pictureships)

the weather. The company policy, which to my mind was an excellent one, was for the Masters to encourage their 1st Officers to develop their expertise in weather conditions appropriate to their level of experience. When I was Master, despite the fact I loved doing it myself, I made it a practice to do all the berthing and unberthing on the first round trip and let the 1st Officer do the second round trip. This practice of course made the transition from 1st Officer to Master far less traumatic than it might have been.

THE *MAID OF ORLEANS* ADVICE ON BERTHING AT BOULOGNE NO. 14

I suppose my fondest memories of my time as 1st Officer are when I was on the *Maid of Orleans*. The Master I was with was a man who did not particularly enjoy ship handling and in consequence let me do the lot, regardless of the weather. He did have some lovely sayings though. When I asked him how to make no.14 berth in Boulogne in a South Westerly gale his reply was, "Drive her in, hit her hard and tie her up while she is

▲ The *Lord Warden* lays by in Boulogne's berth 14 with the *Maid of Orleans* astern in number 15. (John Hendy collection)

◀ With Captain George Sutcliffe in command, the *Maid of Orleans* steams up to her berth on Dover's Admiralty Pier at the conclusion of her final sailing from Calais in September 1975. (John Hendy)

The *Maid of Kent* arrives at Dover Eastern Docks. Built for the Dover – Boulogne service in 1959 she remained in service on the Strait until 1974 when she was transferred to open a new seasonal service between Weymouth and Cherbourg. On 30th October 1981 the *Maid of Kent* operated her final sailing between Weymouth, Jersey and Guernsey. On 24th November she was moved to Newhaven for lay-up pending sale. On 10th April she left Newhaven under tow for San Estaban de Pavia, Spain for scrapping by Desguaces Aviles S.A. (John Hendy)

still stunned"! When you were handling a ship with a bow rudder, this was good advice because once you started to slow down you lost all control of the bow.

It did mean that you had to know your engineers and be able to rely on them to put the steam in to pull you up sharpish when you needed it. We very much depended on one another. The *Maid of Orleans* was a beautiful ship to handle and contrasted with the *St Patrick* which did rather live up to her nickname among the Masters of 'The Black Pig'. She was a ship that you had to drive rather harder than the 'Maid' as she tended to have a mind of her own.

In 1975 I was fortunate again to be relieving the regular Master of the *Maid of Orleans* (Captain Ralph Stanley) for his annual leave when she did her last trip. We sailed from Dover in atrocious conditions and arrived back with the wind at gale force and the seas off the western entrance far too rough to swing outside and enter there. Entering the eastern entrance I swung just inside and went across the harbour stern first around the Prince of Wales' Pier into no.1 berth Admiralty Pier. The five retired Masters and the Marine Superintendent who were all on the bridge with me for the last trip were well impressed with the dear 'Maid's' handling capabilities. That evening we sailed to Boulogne to do a 'Special' the following morning. On arrival in Boulogne I was destined for no.14, in a SW'ly gale. I did it as my old mentor told me, regrettably the dear old retired navy chaps that the port employed as mooring hands were too slow to take my head ropes and I drifted away. Luckily I managed to find just enough room to swing my stern away and get the bow back alongside but our stern was perilously close to the rocks at the base of the quay on the other side. The next morning we entertained our last two passengers, a Doctor and his wife from Folkestone, on the bridge and I included them in the Packet Boat mailing of commemorative covers which I had roughed out for the occasion.

A few days later I took the 'Maid' to Newhaven from where she was taken to Spain for breaking. I did manage to acquire a souvenir or two which I distributed to interested parties.

(Editor's note: Thanks to Captain Sutcliffe, I have one of her brass lifeboat name plates proudly displayed on my bookshelf.)

ANNUAL LEAVE

Another period which I found particularly interesting was when I was relieving Masters for their annual leave. This meant sometimes spending a fortnight on a steam ship with bow rudder and telegraph control of the engines and then a fortnight on a motor ship with bow thrusters and bridge combinator control of variable-pitch propellers; quite different techniques.

Captain Colin Roberts recently reminded me of an incident which I had completely forgotten. He was my 1st Officer on the *Vortigern* when I was bringing her into the ferry dock one night and managed to knock off a couple of piles. It annoyed me to the extent that I voiced my displeasure with myself somewhat colourfully. The Berthing Master, I believe it was Mike Baker, looked up and said, "I am surprised at you Captain, and you a religious man."

Another similar occasion was when I was on the *Dover*. It was my custom, when the visibility allowed, to walk around the ship at least once each watch. One evening sailing I was going through the galley and asked the Chief Cook what was for supper. He replied "Curry". "Lovely," I said, "I love a bit of curry and rice". "Ah well captain" said the cook, "I thought I would put it on tonight with chips instead". I blew my top and said that if he couldn't cook everything in the deep fryer he couldn't cook. I then stormed out! When the supper came up there was rice with it. The next day the Senior Cook was off watch and his assistant who was in charge said to me, "You were angry last night weren't you sir?" "Too right I was," I replied. "Yes I know," he said, "you swore!"

FROM E CREW TO SENIOR MASTER *ST ANSELM*

On arrival back from Newhaven in 1973, where I was relieving on the new *Senlac,* I found that the staff office were regarding me more as a Master who had on occasions dropped back to 1st Officer as opposed to being a 1st Officer who was lucky to get the chance to go out as Master.

Around this time, I was relieving a 1st Officer serving on the *Vortigern*. We were approaching Boulogne and Captain John Arthur was on the bridge. He had brought some papers up with him which he was studying. It has always been my policy to carry on giving orders until the Master said he had the con and I continued to do so on this occasion. When I had given 'stand by' and directed the quartermaster to bring her round for entry, Captain Arthur asked, "Do you want to take her in?" "Certainly sir," I replied. Adding that I had handled the ship before. "When?!" snapped Captain Arthur, surprised that someone had been playing with his precious vessel without him knowing. I explained that with the B crew Master I had taken her in and out of Dunkirk on many occasions. I did the rest of the handling that day and the next morning he announced that he had arranged with the staff office for me to remain with him for formal training as Master when the 1st Officer returned and I was then to remain as D crew Master. I guess I had 'made it'. When he passed me out he put in his letter to the Marine Superintendent: "Captain Sutcliffe has been fortunate enough to have experienced gale force winds during his training." I might have described it differently but as I have said I did enjoy handling – whatever the weather.

It was possibly because of this time with him that Captain Arthur asked for me to join the *St Anselm* as one of his team of Masters when she came in 1980. Joining as E crew Master, by the time I retired ten years later I had spent a year as the ship's Senior Master. One memorable occasion was when we arrived in Dover one evening. A dispute of some sort at the Eastern Docks meant that only cars and foot passengers were allowed off but the freight vehicles were kept on board. We were told to anchor in the harbour until the matter was resolved. I called Snargate Radio and asked if I could take them to Folkestone for discharge. The duty manager said that it was a good idea but the ship had never been to Folkestone. My reply was "I know the ship has never been there but I have been there many times and I can assure you I will enter with the greatest caution". He saw the logic and agreed. We were able to berth in Folkestone although I had to hold the ship at a slight angle to the ramp as she was wider than the ships it had been built to take. We were able to discharge our very grateful drivers. Throughout the ten years I was on the *St Anselm* I don't think I served on any other vessels apart from the *St David* which was with us for a few months in 1982/1983 while the *St Anselm* was away in Belfast having her accommodation extended aft. I took the *St David* on her first trip to Calais, the occasion when John Hendy took a very nice photo of her passing Calais pier heads.

In about December 1989, I was standing in the covered way waiting to board. There was a gale blowing, the ship was late and I knew that I was faced with a night of chasing to get back on schedule, fretting as I waited for other ships to berth. When I got aboard, out came my little portable typewriter and I informed the staff office of my intention to retire on my 60th birthday the following August. When I told my wife on arrival home the next morning her response was, "What have you done? What have you bent?"

I still enjoyed my ship handling and working with people but the odd niggles were beginning to set in, not least among them the job being increasingly run by accountants. And once again good fortune shone upon

Under the command of Captain George Sutcliffe, the *St David* is seen arriving at Calais on her first crossing from Dover. (John Hendy)

me as by retiring early, Mary and I had 16 good retirement years together before she died.

THE BACK DOOR TO DOVER – A TALE OF FRENCH SEALINK

John Hendy

For many years, the quietest and most leisurely Channel crossing was by train ferry from Dunkirk. After the move to the new Port Rapide (Dunkirk West) in 1976, the ships were inevitably busier but by then the first generation train ferries had all gone and the service was being maintained by the French-registered *Saint Eloi* and the elderly *Saint-Germain.*

On a warm Sunday afternoon in May 1984, my colleague Miles Cowsill and I turned up at Dunkirk West for an afternoon crossing to Dover. The

The *Saint-Germain* leaving Dover for Dunkirk in August 1977. (Don Smith/Pictureships)

Captain Bernard Deleplace bringing the *Saint-Germain* into Dover. The Dover pilot is on the left. (John Hendy)

Saint-Germain was on the berth and nothing much appeared to be happening. We joined the queue, if queue it was, and waited. Eventually, just a few minutes before the advertised departure time, a single seaman appeared and waved us forward, up the side ramp and into the ship's garage at the after end of her Promenade Deck.

Built in Denmark in 1951, the *Saint-Germain* was a ship with an abundance of old world charm. Her wooden decks, panelled vestibules and signs asking you to be quiet on the train deck for fear of disturbing sleeping passengers were happy reminders of the fabled 'Night Ferry' service. The leisurely nature of the crossing was re-emphasised a few years later when we were invited to join the Master and officers for lunch on board the *Transcontainer 1*. "When do we depart?" I naïvely asked the Captain. With a shrug of the shoulders he replied, "As soon as we've finished."

It was obvious from the start that all on board held the 'Germain' in great esteem and perhaps her greatest enthusiast was her Master, Captain Bernard Deleplace who gave us the freedom of the ship from wheelhouse to engine room. The Captain constantly emphasised that his was "a *real* ship" and ever appreciative of an audience, decided to swing her outside the western entrance and, using the bow rudder, run the ship astern all the way into the train ferry dock. This unusual manoeuvre ("we practise in case of an emergency") was not entirely successful and at one time it looked as if we were going to berth at the end of the Prince of Wales' Pier. However, following an adjustment, we were soon nestling in the train ferry dock and waiting to be pumped up to the rail level ashore.

And as if one's impressions of this fine ship were not already warm enough, Captain Deleplace then called all the passengers into the forward lounge. Once assembled, he set up drinks asking everyone to toast his ship and the Saint after whom she had been named and whose festival it was on the following day.

A TAXING INTERVIEW

Chief Engineer Chris Davison

In 1985 I applied for a job with Sealink having previously worked as a 2nd Engineer with P&O Normandy ferries out of Dover. When they were taken over by Townsend I decided to take redundancy and try for a 2nd Engineer's job with Sealink.

I had worked a 12-hour shift the night before and finished at 7 am; the interview was arranged for two hours later. I had to report to the clerk at Southern House in Dover who checked my paperwork and the forms I had already filled in. I was then sent to the superintendent in another office in the nearby Packet Yard. Unfortunately he was delayed so my interview didn't start until 10.30 by which time I was pretty tired! I managed to stay awake for all the usual questions relating to the type of machinery I was familiar with and the ships I had worked on. The superintendent was obviously satisfied with me because he soon told me I had got the job and after that I really relaxed. However, he continued talking about the expansion of Sealink and the plans for the future of the fleet at Dover and Folkestone and I found myself nodding off to sleep, only for a few seconds, on a couple of occasions. When he had finished he sent me back to the clerk for my joining instructions. By the time I got to him the first thing he said to me was, "I understand you were a little tired at the interview?" So my claim to fame was I went to sleep at the interview and still got the job! It did me no harm because I finished up as Chief Engineer.

FANTASIA AND THE FRENCH DAY-TRIPPERS

Mike Jackson

I was working on the *Fantasia* when she became responsible for a change in Dover Port routines. Bunkering takes place from bunker barges, usually during the night. With short turnarounds there are times when not all the ordered bunkers can be delivered due to time constraints and so crews and engineers became adept at disconnecting hoses and mooring lines at the last possible moment.

However, one night in the 1990s unmooring the bunker barge was left fractionally too late and the *Fantasia* started leaving the berth with the barge still attached. The ship moved only a short distance with the barge alongside, but questions were asked and thereafter any ship that had been involved with bunkering had to make a report to Port Control that the bunkering operations were completed and the barge disconnected and let go before declaring, "Topline."

We also had a case on the *Fantasia* when the ship arrived in Dover and the traffic embarked only to find a French car unclaimed on the car deck. Unsurprisingly this caused some security concerns and the car was pushed into a corner, taken back to Calais and unloaded where it was lucky not to have been blown-up by the French Security people.

Meantime the Coastguard was advised and shipping asked to look out for swimming Frenchmen.

Later in the day an elderly French couple turned up in the foot passenger check-in in Dover and asked to join a ferry to return to Calais. They were instantly recognised by the computer as the missing driver and his passenger and were asked to explain themselves.

It turned out that they had not previously been on a ferry and had thought that it would be nice to have a daytrip to Dover. Accordingly they had checked-in their car at Calais in the usual manner. Being quite new to the port they followed all the instructions and signs and eventually found themselves in an underground car park. It was a jolly clever car park as it had a lift that took them straight up into the ship!

On arrival at Dover they disembarked with the foot passengers and had a lovely day in Dover, quite unaware of the incident they had caused.

We regularly got complaints from punters sitting in the forward lounge on the *Fantasia* that the ship had left Calais with the bow doors open – this was,

The *Fantasia* arriving at Calais when new. (John Hendy)

of course, the bow visor which could not be lowered until the ship was a few feet out of the berth. I believe that some Masters modified their Calais sailing announcement accordingly to explain this phenomenon. On one occasion the visor lowering was filmed by a passenger and broadcast by Meridian TV, who didn't know any better.

Not only elderly French couples could make mistakes – there was a written complaint one time from a British motorist who was parked on the top deck of the *Fantasia* which was of course open at the stern. When he was sent down to rejoin his vehicle on arrival at Dover the ship was already swung and was proceeding stern-first towards the berth. The motorist assumed that we were proceeding bow-first and that the bow doors were open and had been so all the way from Calais.

One of the girls in Reception claimed that soon after we left Calais on one occasion, an American lady came to the desk and asked, "Excuse me Ma'am, when do we start going through the Channel Tunnel?"

The former Weymouth – Channel Islands mail steamer *Caesarea* took over the Dover/ Folkestone – Calais/ Boulogne train connected services in 1976 and continued to work on a seasonal basis until her withdrawal in October 1980. Under the command of Senior Master, Captain Mike Bodiam, here she is at berth 2 on Dover's Admiralty Pier during July 1976 awaiting her boat trains from London (Victoria) prior to working the 13.00 to Boulogne. (John Hendy)

The main vehicle deck of the *Vortigern* which also shows the four sets of rail lines on Sealink's most versatile vessel. (John Hendy)

Inset: the wheelhouse of the *Vortigern*. (John Hendy)

The *Vortigern* looking her best as she rounds the West Pier at Calais on an afternoon crossing from Follkestone in October 1982. (John Hendy)

The *Vortigern* arriving at Boulogne on her final 'advertised' sailing in September 1986. (John Hendy)

INVICTA

John Hendy

For 26 unbroken years, the *Invicta* was Dover's 'Star Turn' and was always commanded by the local fleet's Senior Master.

Completed by Denny of Dumbarton at the outbreak of war, the *Invicta* was not able to assume her intended service until October 1946, taking over from the *Canterbury* on the fabled London – Paris 'Golden Arrow' link between Dover and Calais. It had been the *Canterbury* that had started the 'Arrow' in May 1929, carrying a maximum of just 300 First Class passengers between Dover's Admiralty Pier and Calais Maritime while the normal service steamer followed 30 minutes behind her. The recession during the early 30s saw the *Canterbury* converted into a two-class ship and the advent of air travel between London and Paris saw some of the service's prestige slip away as the rich, the wealthy and the crowned heads of Europe took to the skies.

Under the command of Captain HL Payne, the *Invicta* was the largest cross-Channel steamer then in service, her extra deck, towering superstructure and elegant funnel making her immediately recognisable. Such was the esteem in which the plain-talking Captain Payne was held that soon after entering service, the *Invicta*'s original bridge wing cabs were removed,

Payne considering them to be a "bloody nuisance"! With his untimely death in the Master's cabin on board the ship during the mid-fifties, the Dover Strait most certainly lost one of its most colourful and most-respected figures.

On 25th April 1963, the *Invicta* officially reopened the western entrance of Dover Harbour which had been closed by blockships during the war. In this day and age her schedules make fascinating reading; leaving Dover at 12.30 each day for Calais, she was back at her berth at 17.30 therefore spending some 19 hours each day in steam at the Admiralty Pier's berth 2. Such a generous timetable could never again be considered but gives a good indication of just how important the 'Golden Arrow' service then was to the railways of Britain and France.

The *Invicta*'s final Master was Captain Elgar Blaxland and it fell to him to take the ship from Dover on her very last crossing of the Dover Strait on a stormy 8th August 1972. Two days later she sailed to Newhaven to lay up eventually passing to Dutch breakers. Of all the turbine steamers to have been engaged on the Dover Strait services, the *Invicta* was the only one to remain on the service for which she was built. The *Maid of Orleans* then took over the running of the 'Golden Arrow' until the end of September 1972 when the link – which was by then but a shadow of its former self – was finally broken. With the new vehicle ferries *Hengist* and *Horsa* in service, the short-sea routes became one class and although the Dover – Calais rail connected services continued on a seasonal basis until September 1993, the end of the *Invicta*'s long innings most certainly marked the closure of a glorious era.

The *Invicta*.
(Don Smith/Pictureships)

Harwich

RECOLLECTIONS FROM THE 60s

Captain Bob Blowers

Having served as a seasonal Second Deck Officer on Townsend Bros. Ferries' 1962-built vessel *Free Enterprise* for the summer of 1964, I had been well and truly bitten by the ferry bug and didn't want to go back to 'deep-sea' sailing again. However, I needed a job for the winter and so applied and gave my details to several of the short-sea companies and the Officers Association. An uninformative telephone call, taken by my father-in-law, brought me to Parkeston Quay, Harwich to join what I had eventually presumed to be British Railways Board's Eastern Region vessels. This proved to be correct and after a very short interview with the personnel man in which I had only to confirm that I had a Master's Foreign Going Certificate I was instructed to join the small container vessel *Colchester* and warned that, as they were between Superintendents, I might be formerly interviewed at a later date – which indeed did occur some weeks later.

At this time the Harwich Eastern Region fleet consisted of the night passenger vessels *Arnhem*, *Amsterdam* and *Avalon*; the train ferries *Suffolk Ferry*, *Norfolk Ferry*, *Essex Ferry* and *Cambridge Ferry*; and the small container cargo vessels *Isle of Ely* and *Colchester*.

My voyage on the *Colchester* was only for what was known as 'makee-learn' or familiarisation purposes and I would have to do similar sailings on a train ferry and a passenger vessel so that in theory I could cover as Second Officer on any class of the vessels if required. Thus in the next few weeks, in between normal duties, round trips were duly completed in the *Essex Ferry* and the *Arnhem* to gain that experience. On the latter vessel, having been aft on leaving Parkeston Quay, I stood at the rear of the Bridge watching points and when passing Harwich town, where a sharp turn was necessary, the Bridge Boy on the engine telegraphs mistook the order for 'half ahead' as 'full ahead' and the 22-knot ship took off like a rocket for a few moments, much to the angry concern of the Captain, until the order was quickly corrected.

One of the disadvantages of the officer manning system in operation at the time was that it was based on rates of pay. Thus the progress of advancement was from Second Officer cargo ship to Second Officer train ferry, Chief Officer cargo to Chief Officer train ferry; Second Officer passenger ship to Chief Officer passenger. Then, ten years or so down the line, after perhaps long service on the Mail Boats, to return to cargo ships as a new Master with no recent experience in smaller ships to help. This first voyage on the *Colchester* duly illustrated the above problem in that a new Master was also doing his first voyage and, due to inadequate familiarisation, embarrassingly had to be 'coached' throughout the berthing operations by the very experienced Boatswain who, by tradition, always acted as helmsman entering or leaving harbour.

I then joined the *Colchester*'s sister ship the *Isle of Ely* (866 gross tons) which ran from Parkeston Quay to Antwerp and Rotterdam as required. This proved a pleasant and interesting experience, except in bad weather, when the all-aft bridge and accommodation block made for an uncomfortable passage. These small ships also had a relatively high speed of 15 knots and so care was necessary to avoid possible damage to ship or cargo. One voyage back from Antwerp was particularly unpleasant with storm force winds and I remember feeling very ill in the small chartroom while passing a

The *Essex Ferry*. (John Hendy)

faltering, late ETA to Parkeston Quay via North Foreland Radio and I wondered whether the sympathetic sounding operator there could sense my discomfort. I later noted that only the scupper-gutted Chief Engineer was looking for breakfast prior to getting into the longed-for shelter of the land. Later, on the train home, I met a passenger who had arrived just after us in the Danish passenger vessel *Winston Churchill* and who had had to sit on his cabin deck to dress himself that morning.

On another occasion, on Christmas Eve, we were due to leave Rotterdam and hoping to be back in Harwich in time to enjoy a Christmas at home. Unfortunately the weather was foggy but the Chief Officer and I were able to encourage the Master in his desire to sail by promising our fullest assistance in navigating the busy waterway to the sea. Fortunately the visibility improved as we got to the coast and we had an uneventful trip back to Harwich where there had been a large dump of snow overnight to make it all look like a beautiful Christmas card scene.

The *Colchester*.
(John Hendy collection)

One of the surprising aspects of working for the Company was that we had almost no direct involvement with the loading of the cargo on the container ships or the train ferries, this being left to the boatswain and deck crew. The Master and Chief Officer decided in advance whether adverse weather conditions precluded containers, or other cargo, being carried on deck, and it was the Second Officer's duty to check ashore and advise if there was any hazardous cargo to be carried. On the passenger ships the officers' duties included supervising the security and stowage of the considerable amounts of mail that was carried.

Although the bigger ships carried a Radio Officer, another unusual responsibility of the Deck Officers was to repair the radars when they needed it – usually by replacing valves etc. with the help of a simple fault finding guide. The Deck Officers therefore mainly maintained the bridge navigational watches at sea in rotation and the Master took over as the ship entered the extensive pilotage waters each end.

A strange peculiarity of navigation on these ships was the old fashioned use of quarter points (e.g. NExE½ E) for steering the ships rather than the

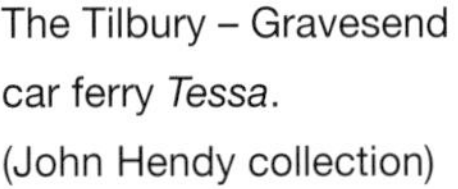

The Tilbury – Gravesend car ferry *Tessa*. (John Hendy collection)

more usual 360 degree compass notation (e.g. 235 degrees) and certainly something I had never seen before or ever really got used to.

Another strange feature of life in the short sea trade at this time was having to pay one shilling and three pence (approximately 6 pence) for each meal which was deducted from the rather low wages each week. The crew received a monthly allowance of various sundry provisions such as tea, sugar butter, cheese and jam which some were known to take home as soon as it was issued and then scrounge whatever extra they could on board.

Smuggling was also rife, amongst certain of the crew at least, as hand rolling tobacco could be bought very cheaply on the other side and sold in the UK at a decent profit. It was said that a random survey of smokers' choices had rated the Belgian 'Drum' tobacco as one of the most popular and yet it was not actually sold in any of the local shops.

One of the duties that very occasionally came the way of a carefully

The *Arnhem* seen from the Avalon at Parkeston Quay – 1964. (John Hendy)

selected Navigation Officer was to 'pilot' either of the two Tilbury-Gravesend car ferries, the *Tessa* and *Mimi* (368 & 463 gross tons), when they had to go to dry dock for annual survey. On one such voyage up to Immingham, the little vessel had proceeded out of an increasingly foggy River Thames with the very unpractised 'pilot' in control and navigating from buoy to buoy by their sound signal as there was no ship's radar fitted at that time. The visibility got steadily worse and finally the 'pilot' decided to anchor for the night as he considered it was too hazardous to continue further. Next morning, before the fog cleared, they could clearly hear the sounds of traffic and even voices fairly close to one side and later as the fog lifted they found they were very skilfully anchored inside the length of Clacton Pier. The little ship's crew were most impressed.

After a couple of months on the *Isle of Ely* I graduated to the *Norfolk Ferry* (3,157 gross tons) where I spent the next three months running between

The *Amsterdam* alongside at Parkeston Quay in 1967. (John Hendy)

Harwich and Zeebrugge. These 14-knot train ferries had a well-deserved reputation for rolling even on a damp lawn, because of their low centre of gravity, but most of my time on there was spent in calm, foggy conditions sailing at the recommended reduced speed. Certainly the older train ferries had no bow thrusts and I remember being very interested that, on berthing at Harwich, the technique was to approach from a right-angle and ram the bow into the soft mud at the end of the quay and then pivot round on this point using the twin screws.

While I was serving at Harwich, because commercial companies were seen to be muscling in on what had always been their trade, the Officers wrote a letter to the Management pledging their support to any attempts to modernise, extend and improve the services operated by the Eastern Region, although I never saw a reply.

I was very grateful to BR for providing me with the perfect opportunity to extend my knowledge and experience of short sea operations and although I had enjoyed my time in the Company, made a number of good friends and I could see there were reasonable career prospects, my gut instinct, which I followed, was to return to Dover where I had been very impressed by the very go-ahead management of Townsend at that time and where a second and larger ship was due shortly and a third even larger ship on order.

(Editor's note: Captain Blowers went on to become Senior Master in the *Pride of Free Enterprise* in 1980 and then the *Pride of Calais* in 1987.)

YOURS IN STEAM!

Philip Cone

As an engineer at Harwich it was required to have a first class certificate of Competency to be appointed 3rd engineer on passenger ships. To be appointed 2nd engineer a combined certificate was required. As the only steamship at Harwich was the *Avalon* I temporarily transferred to Dover to get my steam time in during which time I sailed mainly on the *Holyhead Ferry I* and briefly on the *Dover* and the *Lord Warden*. I was on the *Holyhead Ferry I* when she made her one sailing to St Peter Port.

On one occasion I was on the *Dover* ready to set sail to France; the engine room fully manned and waiting for standby to be rung on the telegraphs. We waited and waited but nothing happened. Eventually the Chief Engineer was getting impatient, he thought there must be some sort of emergency going on so rather than telephone the bridge to find out, he sent the 4th engineer up top to investigate. A few minutes later the engine room telephone rang, it was the 4th to say that the bridge was deserted. The Chief then told him to proceed to the Purser's office as they must be dealing with the "emergency". The 4th proceeded down the bridge ladder and on to the boat deck; again it was deserted. Before reaching the accommodation door he saw a lot of people ashore by the stern of the ship. He went to investigate when they started shouting, telling him to get off, there had been a bomb alert and the ship had been evacuated.

Shame they forgot to tell the engine room!

CRUISING MEMORIES

Philip Cone

The *Avalon* was regularly used for cruising during the spring and autumn months. In September 1971 we sailed out of Casablanca. I (5th engineer) was off watch and had been out on deck watching the ship depart. On

The *Avalon* on a cruise. (Captain Walter Lloyd Williams)

returning to my cabin, along a cross alley way from port to starboard, the ship rolled violently to starboard almost throwing me against the 4th Engineers door and pinning me there until she started to roll to port. I had to hold on to the handrails using all my strength! This was the only time in my seagoing career that I was frightened for the ship and my own safety. Eventually the rolling declined and returned to normal.

At this time the first sitting for dinner had just commenced – most of which ended up on the deck with several stories of near accidents in the galley. Despite several falls and bruises no one was seriously hurt. The biggest casualty was the piano in the 'Deep Sea Dive' bar – it was in pieces over the dance floor. By some miracle the pianist was able to put it together again and play it for the rest of the cruise, though perhaps not fully in tune.

The *Avalon* in the Norwegian fjords. (Will Bramhill Collection)

The *Landguard* dredging at Harwich. (John Wray)

CRUISING PUBLICANS

The *Avalon* was chartered by the Carlsberg Brewery for an educational cruise for publicans, sailing to Oslo and Copenhagen. The only beer permitted to be sold was Carlsberg though the usual spirits were kept on sale. On cruises, the bar usually remained open until about 01.00, then closed until 11.00 the next morning. These publicans were having none of that!

The bar was kept busy that day and the next, continuing until all the Carlsberg had been drunk by arrival in Oslo, along with all the spirits too. The ship was re-stocked in Oslo, again in Copenhagen and was almost dry again on arrival back in Harwich. Extra stewards were drafted in on bar duties with even the chief steward helping out.

SOMETHING DIFFERENT

Captain Trevor Salmon (Holyhead)

One thing deserving mention was the job Captain Alun Thomas and I had for three years running; that of bringing and returning the railway dredger *Landguard* to Holyhead from Harwich. Talk about being hairy!

The skipper Sid was a tough nut cockney and the ship was only intended for harbour dredging. We had to do all sorts of improvisation to cover the coastal passages. Maximum speed was 8 knots and it took us three days with a short refuelling stop at Weymouth. On one trip, Holyhead bound after leaving Weymouth, we started taking in water in the engine room off Portland Bill and only just managed to get back to Weymouth without sinking.

PERFECT BOAT DRILL?

Captain William Bramhill

In any passenger vessel the regulations require that fire and boat drills must be practised and carried out every week and further, they insist that no passenger vessel shall sail without the required number of certified lifeboat men. These certificates are issued by a government institution and are only acquired after a searching examination of the candidate.

My former ship, the *Avalon*, a 6,700-ton passenger vessel, had always managed, due to the complete co-operation of her crew, to muster the smartest official drill in the port of Harwich when the official examiner visited the quay to inspect the state of preparation.

Weeks before the visit, the members of the crew were brought up to peak efficiency by cunning ways which succeeded in holding their interest in an otherwise boring series of drills. The crew did sometimes boast of their achievements, but on one occasion it received the rebuff it deserved.

The examiner arrived on board one fine

Captain William Bramhill. (Will Bramhill Collection)

morning and commanded a drill to commence. Full of confidence the crew set to, dealing first with a simulated fire and then with the preparation of lifeboats. At the given and expected signal of "abandon ship" the boats filled with seamen and rattled down to the water's edge. Soon they were smartly away from the ship's side to be seen rowing hard and with precision down the harbour.

The Chief Officer and I were at the time standing beside the examiner awaiting with smiling expectancy his words of commendation. This morning, however, he remained stony-faced and the Chief Officer, upon whom falls the responsibility for the precision of the drill, shifted uneasily and smiled in such a way that suggested he was about to undergo a spasm of sea sickness. I, the old man, just coughed – the examiner looked at his watch and also coughed – and looked at his watch again.

"Mr Chief Officer," he remarked in icy tones. "You are indeed to be congratulated because your fire drill was excellent and your exercise with the smoke helmets and rescue parties impressed me with its speed, as did the launching of your lifeboats and the quick and efficient way they got clear of the ship."

He gazed into the distance with icy-blue seaman's eyes at the now distant lifeboats. "How far off to you consider those boats to be. Chief?" The Chief Officer who had commenced to preen himself with pride, studied the distant boats with satisfaction. "I reckon they must be at least a mile away by now – my boys are well drilled and can row very smartly when they have to," he said.

The examiner looked at his watch again and then with a quiet snarl he turned his hidden guns on to the grinning Mate. "Yes, fast they are Mr Mate… do you know it is only 11 minutes ago since you sounded the emergency signal and in that time you have managed a fire, a rescue, a passenger assembly at lifeboat stations and boats away… but may I suggest you've moved so fast, you've left all your passengers behind! I am still awaiting your Purser to indicate to me that all passengers are clear of accommodation and mustered at stations."

Then, as though he had willed it, the bridge telephone rang and the Purser's voice came over from the ticket office below, cheerfully announcing all passengers were clear of the accommodation and were now even proceeding to their boat stations. In a withering voice the examiner continued, "Mr Mate, shall we start over again?"

The Chief Officer muttered "Yes" and then retreated very fast, doing in fact a handsome 20 knots down the boat deck towards the ship's bosun!